ROUTLEDGE LIBRARY EDITIONS: CONSUMER BEHAVIOUR

Volume 4

T0362075

CONSUMER EDUCATION

CONSUMER EDUCATION
A Handbook for Teachers

MARION GIORDAN

Routledge
Taylor & Francis Group

LONDON AND NEW YORK

First published in 1980

This edition first published in 2015
by Routledge
2 Park Square, Milton Park, Abingdon, Oxon, OX14 4RN

and by Routledge
711 Third Avenue, New York, NY 10017

Routledge is an imprint of the Taylor & Francis Group, an informa business

British Library Cataloguing in Publication Data
A catalogue record for this book is available from the British Library

ISBN: 978-1-138-79276-0 (Set)
eISBN: 978-1-315-73357-9 (Set)
ISBN: 978-1-138-83914-4 (Volume 4)
eISBN: 978-1-315-73359-3 (Volume 4)
Pb ISBN: 978-1-138-83915-1 (Volume 4)

Publisher's Note
The publisher has gone to great lengths to ensure the quality of this reprint but points out that some imperfections in the original copies may be apparent.

Disclaimer
The publisher has made every effort to trace copyright holders and would welcome correspondence from those they have been unable to trace.

Consumer Education A Handbook for Teachers

MARION GIORDAN

METHUEN LONDON

First published in 1980 by
Methuen & Co. Ltd
11 New Fetter Lane, London EC4P 4EE

© 1980 Marion Giordan
Printed in Great Britain by
Richard Clay (The Chaucer Press) Bungay, Suffolk

British Library Cataloguing in Publication Data

Giordan, Marion
   Consumer education.
   1. Consumer Education – Great Britain
   I. Title
   640.73'07'1041   TX335
   ISBN 0-416-72450-7
   ISBN 0-416-72460-4 Pbk

Contents

1 Introduction   1

2 Consumer education   4
Definitions
The global context
Resources

3 Consumer education in the syllabus   9
Home economics
Design, technology and handicraft
Family and community studies
General studies
Integrated humanities
Economics, government and industrial studies
Commerce and business studies
History
Legal studies
Social sciences, social studies and sociology
Geography
Human biology
Environmental studies
Sciences
English
Communication studies
Religious studies
Non-examination syllabuses
Drama
Degree courses
Vocational training
Pre-retirement courses
Courses for prisoners

4 The consumer   14
Consumer as citizen
Personal interests
Age group
Locality
Motivations
Product availability
Advertising and marketing
Teaching experiences
Resources

5 Shopping   23
The range of shopping opportunities
Services
Where to shop
Shops and their customers
Teaching experiences
Resources

6 Money   32
Where it comes from
Teenage jobs
Pocket money
Methods of payment
Saving
Teenage savings
Teaching experiences
Resources

7 Consumer law   39
Civil law
Criminal law
Teaching experiences
Resources

**8 Consumer protection and consumer
organizations**   49
Government departments

Contents

Government agencies
Local authorities
Consumer organizations
Nationalized Industry Consumer Councils
The European Commission
Consumer representatives
Complaints departments
The media
Teaching experiences
Resources

9 The consumer and the environment   67
Waste and resources
Packaging
Energy
Obsolescence
Some possible solutions
Recycling and reclamation
Conservation
Teaching experiences
Resources

10 More resources and useful addresses   76
General reading
Food
Energy
Labelling
Health and safety

INDEX   78

NOTES   82

1 Introduction

This book has grown out of considerable involvement in consumer education over several years, partly in producing materials for children and information for teachers, partly in dealing with many of the problems people have in adult life when they find themselves ill-equipped to cope with our rapidly changing society.

The framework of the book is based on lectures given at in-service training courses on consumer education at the request of a number of local education authorities, and it incorporates information and resources teachers have found helpful, as well as examples of the way they have incorporated consumer studies in their own teaching. Each chapter thus provides basic information on subject areas related to consumer studies which are demanded in examination syllabuses, some examples of teaching experiences and a list of further resource materials. Since this is a rapidly changing field, and one in which it is essential to keep in touch with the course of events, a number of pages have been left blank at the end of the book for readers to make their own notes of addresses of new organizations, teaching materials and new legislation.

The choice of these resource materials has been deliberately selective. With such a wide-ranging subject as consumer education, I have tried to ensure that the resources mentioned should lead readers on to sources of information where they can find the additional material that interests them. Some are produced by industrial organizations and project their particular viewpoint, which readers will readily recognize, and others by pressure groups or committed individuals, whose perspective is different but equally recognizable. Other sources still are textbooks, government publications, etc. Thus, while you may not always agree with my viewpoint,

you will find sufficient variety among the resources listed here
to provide more information on topics in which you may be
interested.

The basis of the information provided in the book should
also be explained. The material on the way schools and
countries approach consumer education, and on the resources
available in the United Kingdom is based on work undertaken
over a period of years on consumer education projects, which
included co-founding and co-editing a consumer information
newspaper for schools. I was also commissioned by the
Environment and Consumer Protection Service of the
European Commission to report on consumer education in the
United Kingdom under the title 'Education of Consumers: An
Extensive Documentary Search and A Report on Pedagogic
Experiments in the United Kingdom'; the same organization
asked me to organize the EEC Colloquium on consumer
education in schools in the nine countries of the Community,
and to edit the subsequent report. These experiences have
produced useful insights into what teachers need in the way of
information, what children find interesting, the resources
available, and how different countries tackle the subject.

There are many ways of approaching consumer studies. I
have tried to put them in the context of the political, social and
economic framework of the United Kingdom in an attempt to
make the clearest sense of them. The same applies to consumer studies in any country. Most societies seem to reach a
point where pressure to protect, represent, and educate
people as consumers begins to develop. The form that such
developments take in practical terms relates immediately to
the political organization, the economic climate and the society
and traditions of the country itself. This book describes reactions in the United Kingdom to this pressure; other countries
start from a different base and express the same concepts in
different ways. Thus readers from other countries with an
interest in consumer education may find it useful and con-
structive to compare what happens in the United Kingdom
with what happens in their own society.

A great many people and organizations have helped me in

the course of my work in consumer education, and have thus influenced the form of this book. I particularly want to thank those education authorities – particularly the Inner London Education Authority – whose advisers and inspectors have invited me to lecture at seminars and in-service courses on consumer education; those schools where I have been able to talk to children and students about many of the subjects in this book, and the Environment and Consumer Protection Service of the European Commission, for commissioning the work which has given me additional perspectives on the subject.

There are also many colleagues and friends in government departments and agencies, consumer organizations, schools and colleges, who have discussed aspects of consumer education with me, updated my information, and brought resources and schoolwork to my notice, both in the United Kingdom and in other parts of the world. They make a cast of some hundreds, and I am very grateful to them all.

Finally, the intention behind this book. I have written it, having been committed to consumer education for some years, and because I think it should be more widely incorporated in school curricula. From the information it contains, particularly in chapter 3, it must be clear that a consumer perspective can be incorporated in many subjects and at all ages, from nursery school children, as in Belgium, to pre-retirement courses. In time I would like it to become a subject in its own right, incorporating economics, law, mathematics, communications, politics, social studies, design and technology, and ethics, because those are the skills required of adults. Until that happy day dawns, however, I suggest that consumer education has wide-ranging application to most subjects, all students and all abilities.

2 Consumer education

Consumer education can be defined in a variety of ways. Some see it as 'wise buying' information and training in how to budget so as to be able to take as much advantage of the consumer society as possible; manufacturers see it as a way of informing consumers about the benefits of their products to encourage them to buy. Others see the consumer society as a highly organized conspiracy to keep workers docile and uncritical, and consumer education as a means of perpetuating that situation. Others again, of whom I am one, see it as a means of creating and achieving change in society, so that instead of being formed and manipulated by our consumer society, we adapt it to our needs.

These are of course simplistic definitions, but each has its supporters. The definition offered by the International Organization of Consumers' Union is 'critical awareness, social responsibility, involvement or action, ecological responsibility, and solidarity (among consumers)', and this is the interpretation closest to the one on which this book is based.

I see consumer education in the context of the rapidly changing and complex world we live in. It is a world based on and formed by technologies, industries and institutions of which most of us, even in adult life, comprehend only a small part. Consumer education creates awareness of this changing world, of the need for information and guidelines by which one may plot one's way through it, with the least possible personal damage and the means of bringing about change if that appears to be required. Thus consumer education is about asking questions and subsequently making decisions which are as much political as personal.

This is of course what education is about anyway. But consumer education has a particular perspective which casts a light on other aspects of life. The way in which people use money is intensely personal and individual. The way they allocate and spend their resources is in a sense a form of self-expression. The way we use money is the way we create our own particular physical worlds, in terms of what we eat, where we live, what we wear, our interests, our concern for what others think of us. The way we spend money and what we spend it on is the way we operate our lives, and is thus of immense importance and a very fundamental and basic part of our lives. For most of us the material world dominates, and it is our concern — or obsession — because it shows the consumer society in its most selfish and least attractive light.

The way we spend our money is one of the last areas of free choice left to us. There are constraints in every part of our lives: housing, jobs, health, personal relations may be unsatisfactory and show little prospect of improvement in the immediate future. But spending money gives the illusion of control and power, and can also be very enjoyable. It is a means by which we alleviate and furnish the fundamentally harsh conditions of life. That is what makes us vulnerable within the consumer society, and in need of protection against it. It is also something that no one can escape, no matter how high-minded: we all need, at least, food, shelter and clothing, and we can soon add to that list many other items; medical services, transport, sanitation, education, money and so on.

Moreover the choice we thought was free is not free at all. We are buying other people's decisions, just as our lives in relation to other physical and material matters such as housing, jobs, money and transport are formed by other people's decisions. Products in the market place are largely structured to use existing materials, to be made on available machinery, designed and packaged to travel long distances within the existing distribution network, and to fit in with retailers' arrangements. Moreover our desires for these products are, in my view, highly manipulated by manufacturers, retailers, and their advertising agents, to encourage us, not just to want them but to feel they are essential to our well-being. On this premise is the industrial society based.

Now as well as wanting to know how to work your way through this maze, you also have to live and work in it. It brings many benefits, as well as hazards and exploitation. We in the United Kingdom also live in a parliamentary democracy, and we may wish to change our society's institutions or take part in the decision-making process, since as well as being consumers we are also citizens. Thus consumer education is advice for living, and moreover for living with change and perhaps creating change.

THE GLOBAL CONTEXT

The growing interest in consumer education is not by any means confined to the United Kingdom. It has become a world-wide concern, though the way it is taught is related, as always, to the precepts and philosophy of each country's society. In the United States it is perhaps at its most advanced, and in some states is mandatory, and in some high schools a very popular subject. The concepts behind the teaching are closely related to the American outlook of making the best of a fundamentally exploitative society: 'how to avoid the rip-offs', as one boy said.

In French and West German secondary schools consumer education tends to appear in craft and economics courses. The Scandinavian outlook is one that is alert to world needs and resources, particularly to the dehumanizing dangers of con-centrating on consumption as an end in itself. These concepts, on which the experimental Malmö Project in Scandinavian schools is based, start with nine-year-olds, and it includes emotive aspects, like pleasure in buying presents for others. The Belgians have a consumer education experiment aimed at encouraging consumer awareness among nursery school children from the age of three, who learn, for example, about sweets and tooth decay and are encouraged to develop a preference for apples.

The European Commission adopted a commitment to con-sumer education in 1975. It has commissioned reports on the state of the art in different member countries. It held a colloquium in 1977 in London to find out what was happening in schools in member countries, and then prepared teaching materials for trial in schools within the Community.

But in certain European countries such as Ireland, Spain and Portugal, consumer activists have difficulty in getting recognition for consumer education. In those countries consumer awareness is still in its infancy, in many respects and consumer education even further off.

However certain Third World countries concern themselves with consumer education in ways which relate very immediately to their own circumstances. In the Philippines, for example, consumer education is teaching people to boil water before they drink it, and to examine sugar for impurities – both products we in the United Kingdom and similar economies take for granted as being fit and wholesome for immediate consumption.

In the United Kingdom, the interest in consumer education has come from the consumer organizations and central and local government as much as from teachers anxious to protect children from the impact of the exploitative nature of the consumer society. The Welsh Consumer Council and the National Federation of Consumer Groups are active in consumer education, as are some local authority consumer protection departments. Other initiatives have come from the Department of Prices and Consumer Protection and its successor, the Consumer Affairs Division of the Department of Trade, from the Department of Energy, the Office of Fair Trading in its consumer information activities, the British Standards Institution, the Electricity Consumers' Council, and others, possibly perceiving not only the need for consumer education but also that it might be a more effective way to protect consumers than laws and institutions. Whether these consumer education efforts will ever replace the need to protect people in these ways is of course unlikely.

Resources

Report of the 1977 Colloquium on Consumer Education in Schools in

the Community, ed. Marion Giordan (Commission of the European Communities: Brussels, 1980).
Educating the Consumer, Alma Williams (Longmans, 1975). (0 582 36507 4(pb); 0 582 36310 1 (hb))*
Reading, Writing and Relevance, Mary Hoffman (Hodder & Stoughton, 1976). (0 340 21025 7)
Reading and the Consumer, Alma Williams (Hodder & Stoughton, 1976). (0 340 21027 3)

The two latter books contain useful descriptions of using consumer information in teaching, and are set books for the Open University course in Reading Development PE 231, on the teaching of reading, which itself contains some stimulating units on e.g. advertising.

---

* Throughout the book ISBN numbers are given where relevant.

3 Consumer education in the syllabus

There is, at the time of writing, no examination syllabus in the United Kingdom called 'consumer studies' or any similar name. Nevertheless, topics with consumer relevance appear in many O level, A level, CSE and Scottish syllabuses, while consumer affairs can be used to illuminate and give a deeper perspective to many others which may be less immediately obvious. Because syllabuses vary from one examining board to another, it is not possible to point to particular subjects and be confident that they all contain the same sections or units. However, from the point of view of their consumer studies content, some syllabuses seem to group themselves. Thus this brief chapter is not an exhaustive list of the examination syllabuses which include some aspect of consumer studies, but a kind of overview as to where this occurs in some form, and to which the material contained in this book is relevant.

Home economics almost invariably contains sections or units on money management, consumer guidance, consumer protection and redress, shopping, product standards and safety, consumer organizations and advertising, and aspects of consumer law such as labelling. Related subjects, like needlecraft and textiles, and food and nutrition, often call for knowledge of the same kind of information, for example about consumer groups, the Fibre Content Regulations, the Office of Fair Trading Code of Practice on launderers and dry-cleaners, or the Labelling of Food Regulations and the Food and Drugs Act.

Many *design*, *technology* and *handicraft* subjects are taught with a consumer bias, even though the syllabus does not always give that lead; however in view of the consumer implications of these subjects, a consumer perspective ought to be included. Consumer studies are almost tailor-made for design syllabuses with units such as: 'studying the needs of the elderly in the design of products', 'ways of improving the design of kitchen equipment or modern furniture', and many others related to the appropriate use of materials.

Related syllabuses, like *family and community studies*, can have an option on problem-solving which is strongly consumer-orientated: others, like *general studies*, contain units on 'materials in the service of man', the 'application of art' and the 'economic implications of science and technology', for all of which consumer studies are relevant and indeed essential. *Integrated humanities* is another subject which can have a considerable weighting towards consumer affairs, including shopping, sales promotion and consumer protection and which requires a consideration of planned obsolescence and waste.

Economics syllabuses, particularly those leaning towards social economics, and the broader syllabuses like *government, economics and commerce, economic and public affairs* and *industrial studies*, contain units on living standards, consumer behaviour, the wants and needs of the individual and society, consumer protection, on people as producers, consumers and earners, on profit, manufacturing and the retail trade, and on the social and environmental impact of business enterprise, including waste of finite resources and conservation.

Commerce and business studies can cover some of the same ground, as well as marketing and advertising, obsolescence and the effect of consumer legislation and government controls on business (also to be found in government and politics syllabuses). They tend to include money and credit, the retail trade and consumer protection. These subjects also often include units on pressure groups and their activities, and the inter-relationship between voluntary groups, local authorities, government agencies and central government. Some modern *history* syllabuses cover this ground too, as well as another topic which appears in many of these syllabuses — the effects of mass-communication. Syllabuses on *legal studies* cover contract, civil and criminal law, and in particular the consumer and the law. Quite commonly this group of subjects includes aspects of government and social decision-making.

Social sciences, social studies and *sociology* can contain units on work, youth culture, peer group pressures, reference groups, the changing role of the family, the influence of the media, consumption and standards of living, the allocation of resources, status in society and a number of other aspects such as pressure groups which are either related directly to consumer studies or can be illustrated by them.

Another group of syllabuses with consumer implications includes subjects such as *geography, human biology* and *environmental studies*, with topics such as the built environment, the shape of towns, and transport and distribution systems, all of which are affected by the development of consumer activities like shopping and leisure. Conservation, waste, the use of finite resources, particularly energy resources, are often included, as are related subjects like public health and environmental health.

Science syllabuses, including subjects such as *physics, general science* and *applied science and technology*, often cover energy, energy conservation and loss, nuclear power, electricity, design of electrical appliances, and other aspects related to consumer education and of increasing concern to consumers.

English papers often have questions on advertising, while syllabuses naturally lay much stress on clarity and comprehension — not always apparent in many forms of consumer information like instruction leaflets and hand-books, fuel bills, or government leaflets, all of which are useful exercises in communication — and too often in non-communication. Indeed syllabuses such as *communication studies* emphasize the use of language by business and government. Since many consumer problems arise through poor communications, and since the consumer movement has been closely linked with the media, consumer studies are relevant here as well.

Finally, *religious studies*. These syllabuses quite often contain sections on moral issues, or contemporary issues taken from a moral or ethical standpoint. Examples are conservation, the use of money and leisure, the family in society, work, profit, wealth – all aspects of consumer studies.

While this is not an exhaustive list, it could be pursued almost indefinitely through CSE (particularly Mode 3), O levels and A levels.

There is also a good deal of consumer education in *non-examination syllabuses*, particularly in the first and second years of secondary school, in middle schools, and in project work in primary schools, where making up cosmetics and toiletries at a fraction of the market price, comparing prices, preparation times and results of convenience foods, and counting crisps or sweets in packets and working out the unit price, are popular exercises.

A good deal of consumer education also goes on in the teaching of drama, when, for example, role-playing is used in consumer situations like choosing, buying and taking back an item, or in finding out where to complain. This is often not only a learning process, but also one which gives students confidence (see p.47).

Several degree courses in home economics have a strong consumer education bias, as do marketing degree courses, management studies and some law degree courses. In vocational training there can be consumer education elements in engineering apprenticeship courses, nursery nurse training courses, and many others, while in adult education there are courses run by the Co-operative Union, the Workers' Education Association and the Open University (who produce the *Consumer Decisions* and *Energy in the Home* short courses).

Some companies and local authorities run pre-retirement

courses which include health, housing and money management – all aspects of consumer education. Certain prisons provide courses for prisoners shortly before release on credit and money management – particularly relevant for this group, who may well be serving sentences for financial mismanagement and its consequences. Some prisons extend these courses to prisoners' wives.

However, the number of these teaching initiatives should not be used as grounds for complacency about the spread of consumer studies in the United Kingdom. While many are teaching it, possibly without even realizing it, its impact particularly by comparison with the impact of advertising, that other great consumer education exercise, is still very slight.

4 The consumer

Consumers can be defined very widely. They are consumers of goods and services: that is where the conventional definition rested for a long time. Today, however, they are also recognized as consumers of housing, the National Health Service, the local social services, education, transport and road services, gas, electricity and the postal services, local authority services like waste collection and street cleaning, and government programmes like the motorway network. They are, of course, consumers of the environment, political institutions, pressure groups, and much more. With this breadth of definition, one begins to understand why in some countries, Japan for example, 'consumer' is equated with 'citizen'.

PERSONAL INTERESTS

Moreover, while consumers have this wide general range of interests, particular groups have particular concerns. Food and fuel prices are of interest to people running a home and shopping for themselves or their families, but of even greater interest to people on low incomes, who spend a correspondingly greater percentage of their incomes on them. Cars, petrol prices, servicing and repairs and the condition of roads are all of considerable interest to car drivers, while the standard, frequency and cost of bus services is, naturally, of greater interest to people who travel by them.

AGE GROUP

Apart from personal interests, age is one of the strongest factors differentiating consumers and their interests: the requirements of babies, teenagers, parents and the elderly for shelter, clothing, transport, entertainment and all the other goods and services available vary very considerably according to their age.

For example, teenagers still at school, living at home, perhaps with a part-time job and/or pocket money, may have a considerable amount of spare cash to spend on records, snacks, clothes and shoes, outings to discos, concerts, sports events. Among their priorities may be novelty, fashion, change, low cost, and products which are popular among their group of contemporaries. Housing, food and fuel costs do not concern them, nor do they have to allocate any of their money to feed, clothe and shelter anyone else. Theirs is all personal spending.

Their parents, on the other hand, are more likely to be consumers of household goods and furniture, food and clothing for the whole family, including the teenager, housing, family transport, family holidays, gas and electricity, as well as paying part of their income in taxes which can include television licence, road fund licence and rates and national insurance, as well as income tax. Their demands and concerns being quite different, their financial constraints are bound to be correspondingly greater.

The elderly pensioner is a different type of consumer again: spending less on household goods, more on warmth, less on personal transport but more on public transport, less on taxes, using the social services more and the educational services hardly at all. Elderly pensioners also buy different products: clothes, shoes, and perhaps even different food. These differences are not entirely to do with lower income: not all pensioners are poor. But there is evidence that people's choice of goods does vary in some respects according to their age group.

LOCALITY

Consumers also vary according to where they live: town and country seem still to be strong dividers. People in remote areas have particular needs for transport and such problems as, for example, access to doctors and dentists. Their shopping habits may be different, with a greater reliance on mail order, and they may pay more and have less choice than people in towns. They may also have less access to advice services, so that their consumer problems may be doubly difficult to solve.

MOTIVATIONS

Most consumers can be defined according to age, special concerns, locality, family structure and income. These are the main *conscious* parameters for most consumers who are united in wanting shelter, warmth, food and clothing, but have varying amounts of money, varying numbers of people to provide for, different needs for goods and services, and different opportunities for acquiring them in terms of time, transport and availability of shops. These are the motivations and factors which should make being a consumer a logical, rational process. If they were the only factors affecting consumers, it would be possible, for example, for choice to become almost a computerized activity. If that were so, information about a woman of sixty-five who wanted to buy a pair of shoes could be fed into a computer, with information about the type of wear she meant to give them, distance from local shops, money she wanted to spend and range of styles available; the answer would be the logical choice for someone of her age, habits, locality and income. All very rational, but what about taste? She might not like them, and would have foregone the pleasure, sometimes a dubious one, of looking for the shoes and making up her mind. Apply that example to a fifteen-year-old looking for fashion shoes, and the absurdity of the situation becomes even more apparent.

There is a dimension to being a consumer ignored by considerations of logic and practicality: the dimension of the *unconscious* motivations which are part of every personality, and which makes them individuals. The way people spend their money is an expression of personal choice, of what they want to make of their lives; an expression of self. In every aspect of spending money, as opposed to the occasions when money is spent for you by, for example, local and national government, over which you have little apparent control, there is a strong element of the irrational.

These unconscious motivations are varied. Any group of teenagers, in telling you why they bought a particular pair of shoes, can demonstrate that they did not buy them simply to keep their feet warm and dry or to protect them. They bought them to look taller, because other people of their age had something similar, because they wanted to look tough or smart – they have all kinds of reasons, a combination of peer group pressures and fashion, fantasy and that special indefinable something about the shoes that appealed to them and made them buy. Adolescents are of course not alone in this.

A great deal of money spending is affected by the desire to show off, to demonstrate prestige, to show that one is smarter, better and essentially 'different' from other people. In a world of mass-produced goods and services and institutions catering for large numbers of people where products, services, education, health treatment, forms of transport, and work conditions are widely similar, patterns of spending money are what we use to distinguish ourselves from other people. Walk along a row of very similar houses, and you will see that every front room is different, so is every garden, and so are the inhabitants and their car. What makes them all different is the way they have spent their money.

These unconscious motivations are what makes spending money such an absorbing interest to most people, and the way other people spend their money equally absorbing and fascinating. For what do we frequently talk about but the way our friends and colleagues dress, furnish their homes, eat, entertain themselves, and travel? And how often do we speculate about how much they have spent on something and how much they have to spend? One discussion into which school children will throw themselves with enthusiasm, interest and considerable knowledge is about their spending money, where it comes from, and where it goes.

PRODUCT AVAILABILITY

But having said that, there is yet another important dimension to being a consumer: what is available for us to spend our money on. We choose to spend it among a relatively limited range of goods and services – limited by technology, by materials, engineering and design, and limited most of all by the decisions of manufacturers and retailers as to what they can provide for us. When we buy the products we see displayed on shop shelves, these are the results of production and design decisions by manufacturers, as well as being the results of decisions by the retailer to stock them. The same applies to services: banks, post offices and building societies provide a great many high street and shopping centre outlets where we can deposit and draw our money. Any changes in the service they decide to offer will be affected by the historic fact that they already have money tied up in shopping street sites and in staff just as much as by consumer preference. Similarly, any manufacturer considering a new product will bear in mind his own plant and the expertise of his staff just as much as whether consumers have shown the slightest interest in the new product.

ADVERTISING AND MARKETING

This leads on to another dimension affecting the consumer: advertising and marketing. How else do we find out about new products and services if not by advertising? It is an information system, in the way that station signs advertise the presence of a transport system, car names advertise the name of the manufacturer and the model, and the sign outside a shop advertises the shop itself. This informative element in advertising is often overlooked. A considerable percentage of all advertising is classified advertising, mainly for jobs and for homes and businesses; in 1978, out of a total of £1,834 million spent on advertising, 22 per cent was spent on classified advertisements. Another 2 per cent went on metrication and fuel conservation.

However, the advertising that attracts most attention is for goods and services. In 1978, 40 per cent of advertising expenditure was on consumer products (known as Manufacturers' Consumer Advertising) and 17 per cent went on retail advertising. This expenditure is visible in television and radio commercials, newspaper and magazine advertisements, on packaging and labels, vans, posters, carrier bags, and many other places. But although it may seem to be indiscriminate, it is not. Like products and services, advertising is carefully aimed at the target groups most likely to be prepared to pay for them. Snack foods are aimed at teenagers who have the spare cash and the appetites for them; advertisements for snack foods are therefore designed to appeal to teenagers and appear in places where teenagers are most likely to encounter them, like teen magazines, and commercial radio stations. More subtly, products with a good deal of competition but little noticeable difference between them are promoted to particular sectors of the market: e.g. the luxury high-technology car for the high-flying executive or person who likes to think he is one, and the sporty small foreign car for the younger buyer who prides himself or herself on being a go-getter, no-nonsense kind of person – or would like to be seen as that kind of person. Advertisements will be in the specialist car magazines, in Sunday supplements, in the so-called 'quality' newspapers and on television, where car buyers or people who run company cars are likely to see them.

The effect of this dimension of advertising and marketing is to feed many of the fantasies previously mentioned, to create images (for example of women as being happily employed at housework), to stimulate desires (for example, for a newer, better washing machine) and obviously to inform consumers where needs can be met (by telling them where a bus station is or where they can buy jam).

These are the factors which provide an answer to the complicated question: what is a consumer? We are of course all consumers, but our needs vary according to age, income, and circumstance, and our desires vary even more widely. Moreover, as consumers we are part of the economy in which we live, part of the society, and also part of the political structure – all roles which are more fully explored in later chapters.

The way teachers decide to identify the consumer and consumer demands focus mainly on teenage spending, products of particular interest to teenagers, and the advertising aimed at them.

A collection of advertisements cut out of teen magazines produces plenty of material about the areas where teenagers feel most vulnerable – their hair (shampoos and conditioners), skin (products claiming to clear spots and acne or to 'improve' the complexion in some way), smells (deodorants and perfume) – all of which have an underlying theme of lack of confidence and are, incidentally, of as much interest to boys as to girls. This kind of advertising has been used for exhibitions on advertising and marketing to teenagers to heighten awareness of their role as consumers and as a special target for advertisers.

Many teachers also use particular magazines, e.g. those aimed at elderly women, or at affluent young to middle-aged readers, and work out a readership profile with the class. Others get pupils to monitor television advertisements over a period of time and then to analyse the products and the frequency and times at which they are advertised.

Some home economics teachers have structured lessons around shampoos and hairdryers by getting as many as possible in the class to bring their own and to wash and dry each other's hair, learning how the products differ as well as how their own requirements and reactions differ, thus focusing on the varying demands consumers make as well as on product comparison. It obviously requires considerable organization and it is only fair to say that some teachers have reacted with horror on hearing about it, although those who have tried it regard it as their most successful lesson ever.

Advertising aimed at teenagers, and teenage exploitation by the pop music world and fashion industries, are popular sub-

jects for drama. Hainault High School first years produced
Rikky, a dramatic event built round the rise and fall of a singer,
and the exploitation of teenagers by record promoters.

Resources

In the main these are suggested as background reading for
teachers and students in higher education.

Consumer as citizen

Real Money, Real Choice: Consumer Priorities in Economic Policy,
National Consumer Council (1978). The first consumer state-
ment on economic policy. (0 905653 15 7)
The Consumer and the State, National Consumer Council (1979).
The second statement, looking at public spending and taxa-
tion.
*The Social Audit Consumer Handbook: A Guide to the Social
Responsibilities of Business to the Consumer*, Charles Medawar
(Macmillan, 1978). (0 333 21665 2(hb); 0 333 21666 0(pb))

Different types of consumer

The Female Consumer, Rosemary Scott (Associated Business
Programmes, 1976). Market research figures on the buying
power of women compared with their low-key status in
advertisements. (0 85227 044 5)

Why the Poor Pay More, ed. Frances Williams (Macmillan and
the National Consumer Council, 1977). (0 333 23644 0(pb))

Advertising and marketing

The IBA Code of Advertising Standards and Practice. Independent
Broadcasting Authority, 70 Brompton Road, London SW3 1EY.
Rules covering television and commercial radio advertise-
ments. Free.
The British Code of Advertising Practice. Advertising Standards
Authority, Brook House, Torrington Place, London WC1E
7HN. Rules covering newspaper, magazine, poster and
cinema advertisements.

Advertising: Legislate or Persuade? National Consumer Council (1977). (0 905653 11 4)

Images of Women: Advertising in Women's Magazines, Trevor Millum (Chatto & Windus, 1975). Analysis of the way women are presented in magazine advertising. (0 7011 2010 X)

How to be Exploited, Marion Giordan (Temple Smith Ltd, 1978). Chapters on marketing and advertising of food, shampoos, deodorants and products for teenagers. Also deals with many aspects of the consumer as a citizen. (0 85117 1400 (pb))

The Hidden Persuaders, Vance Packard (Penguin, 1957). Classic exposé of American advertising methods. (0 14 020585 3)

What Advertising Does, Institute of Practitioners in Advertising, 44 Belgrave Square, London SW1X 8QS. Advertising industry's description of its role. Free.

The Launch of Persil Automatic, Market Research and Advertising, Business Studies Series, Unilever Educational Publications, PO Box 68, Unilever House, London EC4P 4BQ. Interesting account of industry's activities.

Find Out About Advertising, Forbes Publications Ltd (for Advertising Association). Teaching kit produced by the advertising industry.

5 Shopping

The retail trade is acutely aware of the multiplicity of types of retail outlet; consumers are far less so. Yet these differences have a considerable effect on what they pay, what they buy, and the conditions in which they shop. It can also have some effect on whether their consumer problems are easy or difficult to solve.

There is a basic distinction between *self-service* and *counter-service*: with the former goods are displayed on shelves or racks and the customer walks around selecting goods, carrying them to a cash point and paying there, often packing them as well. Usually, though not invariably, self-service will have fast-moving, low priced stock, and staff who display the goods while others operate the cash registers. The goods are pre-packed and price-marked. You are unlikely to get personal service or advice. This is commonly the system on which supermarkets, superstores and hypermarkets are run; the names simply imply a difference in size.

Counter-service implies sales staff who provide some degree of personal service to customers, by weighing out the food they want, bringing clothing forward for them to try on or look at, helping them to try on shoes and subsequently taking the money and wrapping the goods. Customers expect sales staff to be knowledgeable about the goods they are selling, but this is not always the case. You may pay more, but you may be prepared to in order to get some guidance and advice, or, in the case of the corner shop or independent shop, some chat and conversation. Many shops in fact operate a combination of both self and counter-service.

Multiples are chains of stores with a strongly emphasized shop name, much the same selection of goods whichever branch you go into (though there will be some regional variation), and you will find them in shopping centres and high streets right across the country. Well-known names are Woolworths, Boots, Marks and Spencers, British Home Stores, Tesco, Fine Fare and others. A distinguishing feature is their décor: wherever you are in the country you will know you are in a Woolworths or Boots, partly from the stock, but also from the layout, lighting and appearance of the place. These multiples will be almost entirely self-service.

Some multiples specialize: Curry's in electrical goods, Manfields, Trueform and others of the British Shoe Corporation in shoes. Where there is a specialism, there is likely to be a combination of self-service and personal service.

Because multiples usually operate central buying policies and have a great number of outlets, prices can be on the low side. But as they must be sure of mass sales in order to carry any item, special or unusual products may be hard to find.

Specialist shops stock goods within particular categories which, they hope, you will not find elsewhere. Examples are dress shops, craft shops, book shops, delicatessen, gift shops, garden centres. This is the kind of shop where you might hope to find fairly esoteric goods – candle-making equipment, ethnic clothes, imported children's clothes, imported or locally made pottery. You may pay more there than elsewhere, but you expect a higher level of personal service, advice, and interest in you as a customer. Part of the higher price pays for that personal element, part of it is for having a particular kind of stock brought together in one place for you to choose from, and part of it is to allow a return on stock which the proprietors expect to have on their hands for some time.

Department stores are a mixture of the specialist shop and the multiple; there will be departments specializing in, for example, glassware, carpets and electrical appliances, and you ought to get a wide choice, somewhere between the multiple and the specialist shop. Prices, speaking very generally, may also be somewhere in the middle, because you pay for personal service, advice, free delivery and the range of goods. A department store is likely to be one of a chain and to derive some benefit from its buying policies; it is not likely to want to have stock on its hands for a long time and thus may not stock the more unusual goods.

Discount stores have sprung up over the past few years, often to sell household goods and equipment. They cut prices by stocking a limited range of very popular items they know they can sell quickly. The premises may not be very grand – possibly an old warehouse – and you probably pay extra for delivery. You are also unlikely to get much specialist advice from the staff. Choice will be from a range of samples, and you take away or have delivered a sealed container with your purchase. However, consumer laws apply to these purchases just as they do to other consumer transactions.

Cash and carry is a wholesale operation for retailers, small businesses, canteens, etc. Unlike the big multiples who get their stock direct from the manufacturers, small corner shops cannot handle those big quantities and may prefer to get smaller amounts from a cash and carry.

Entry is usually restricted to local traders with a special identification card; people who get in without one can be regarded with some animosity as taking trade away from local shopkeepers. However prices may not be particularly low and, more important, these are not consumer sales, so imperfect, damaged, or unsafe goods can be difficult to get put right.

Market stalls are another place to look for low prices. They might offer fresh produce like fruit, vegetables, eggs and fish which are fresher, cheaper and in better condition than you can get elsewhere. In some areas stalls sell end of lines, off-cuts or seconds from local factories and mills. Selling craft work is a growing trend.

Prices are low because the stall holder's overheads are low and he has to clear his stock by the end of the day. Teenagers are often attracted to market stalls because of the bargains in clothing they can find there, but they can also have consumer problems with the stall holder when something is faulty and they try to take it back.

Mobile vans, on the other hand, are likely to be more expensive. They usually operate in remote country areas and sometimes on large housing estates. For reasons of space their stock is limited and because of the high element of convenience, prices are likely to be higher than in a local town.

Milk floats are mobile shops of a kind offering a very limited range of goods – chickens, bread, cheese, butter, cream, as well as milk – while providing a very high degree of convenience, especially for house-bound people.

Farm shops have grown up over recent years to sell their own produce to passers-by; this makes a pleasant reason for an outing in the car, especially when you forget to add in the cost of petrol and depreciation of the car to the price of a freshly picked cabbage which would make it outrageously expensive. Shopping at farms to buy fruit and vegetables in bulk, often where you can pick your own, has become a recognized cheap way of stocking up a freezer: again it adds an element of pleasure, the knowledge that the food is fresh, and the thrill of an apparent bargain, provided you don't add in the cost of your own labour and the car.

Some farms offering these facilities have got into trouble with local trading standards departments when they have added bananas and grapefruit to their 'home-grown' goods. Farmers who slaughter animals to sell direct to customers for their deep freeze have also been criticized by environmental health officers, because the conditions in which the animals are slaughtered and the animals themselves are not subject to health regulations or inspection, and there could be a health risk.

We have still not covered all the ways in which we can shop. The rest listed here are means of buying and selling products, but they combine a strong service element as well, because the sales can be conducted at home.

Mail order is a very popular way of buying goods. It accounted for a turnover of £2275 million in 1979, or 4.7 per cent of total retail sales for the big mail order companies which sell through their catalogues placed with agents all over the country. This is a form of shopping which is very popular with teenage girls who very often know personally the local agent who holds the catalogue.

Some selling is done at the door, by what is called *doorstep selling*, but this is increasingly frowned on and suspected (with reason) of being high-pressure selling to which housebound housewives and elderly people are particularly vulnerable. In a different category are agents of *direct sales companies*, who call at the house, take orders for their goods and collect the money when they deliver the goods, thereby allowing a cooling-off period. Avon cosmetics are a notable example, and very popular among schoolchildren.

Party selling is a type of direct selling which has come in for criticism, particularly when 'guests' feel they have been under pressure to buy so that their 'hostess' might get a better present from the company's agent for her co-operation. Nevertheless, like all home-buying operations, it provides a chance to handle and choose goods without going far from home, which is valuable for those tied to the house.

The *tallyman* is another trader who calls at the home, and whose activities are little known and not always regarded with approval. Descendants of the old packmen or pedlars, today's tallymen offer goods for sale at so much per week. Research by the National Consumer Council has shown that the goods could have been bought more cheaply in local shops, and that purchasers rarely knew the real price they had paid, which in many examples was far greater than local prices. However, because they are offering credit, tallymen have to be licensed under the Consumer Credit Act, of which more in chapter 7.

Finally there are *second-hand shops*, some elevated to the status of antique shops or Oxfam shops. There are also *jumble sales* and *auctions*. They all perform a valuable function in recycling goods, and providing outlets for both the most valuable and the least valuable goods, which someone will want. Goods sold in this way, including auctions, are not covered by consumer law, unless there has been a case of misleading description, e.g. a second-hand car sold with a mileage far less than it has actually done, or a modern piece of furniture sold as an antique. *Private sales*, e.g. between one person and another and not in the course of their business, are not covered by consumer law either.

SERVICES

Service outlets, offering to sell a service rather than a product, are invariably more highly specialized than retail outlets selling products. They also provide a considerably higher degree of personal attention. Typical examples are cafés, travel agents, banks, hairdressers, dry cleaners, television rental firms, building societies, cinemas, betting shops, and post offices. They all offer to do something for you that you would find it difficult to do for yourself, like booking tickets, cutting your own hair, keeping your money safely.

There is seldom any overlap between those activities, in that a bank will offer to look after your money but will not sell you a holiday. Moreover, while activities like banking and building societies are undertaken almost entirely by large enterprises, others, like dry cleaning, hairdressing, and repairs of various kinds are often undertaken by small individual enterprises.

This service element in shopping is less highly structured than the retail element, and therefore less easily explained in terms of what you can expect to pay for. Moreover, services are the growth area in our society. The more advanced a society becomes, the greater the amount of income allocated to services. As far as consumer education is concerned, we will see (Chapter 7) that while products are relatively well covered by consumer legislation, services are not, and this is where problems can arise.

WHERE TO SHOP

Shops are to be found in high streets, shopping centres, town centres, housing estates, villages, and around markets. They tend to cluster around one another and around a transport system, such as a main road. Their precise dynamic is not clear – why should there be shops in one part of a town and not another?

Shops also tend to attract other shops and services, like buses, banks, car parks, cafés, betting shops and a post office. When a new shopping centre is planned, much importance is given to the right 'mix'; thus other retailers already on the site will express satisfaction when certain other retailers, like a butcher or a greengrocer open a shop. They often say that this means that a 'balance' among outlets has been created. What they really mean is that a consumer coming into the shopping area for one thing is likely to buy something else as well. It is all part of boosting sales.

SHOPS AND THEIR CUSTOMERS

Shopping facilities reflect local needs and demands, local salary ranges, the age of local people, property, and regional tastes. But which comes first: shops or people? The answer is never clear and changes all the time.

For example, an area with a mixture of large and small shops, representing many of the big multiples plus perhaps a street market or a covered market, a post office, gas or electricity board showrooms, betting shop, banks, building society and travel agents can cater for a population of working people and their families who want a wide range of goods and services at competitive prices, related to local income levels and expectations. An upmarket nationally known store will not last long in an area with high unemployment; a cut-price retailer in an affluent area will soon find that he can charge higher prices and get away with it.

But whatever the character of the shopping area, it will attract transport services like buses and car parks, and it will attract customers who want the goods and services they can get there. The shops may have opened because there was a market for their goods, but being there continue to attract shoppers to the area and, in time, other shops.

The actual size of the shops, the transport facilities and the quality of local shopping services partly depends also on the age of local property, on whether new building has been possible, or whether the premises are older and smaller than retailers generally prefer today.

Another interaction between shops and their customers is bound to be the local population. The shops, services and goods available in a prosperous south-east England suburb will be different from those in a down-market Glasgow suburb. Similarly, there are many areas in large cities where ethnic foods can be bought. Originally they catered for local communities; once established they attracted others who want to buy these ethnic goods. These may appear to be extreme cases, but they highlight this very interesting and never answered question about the relationship between the customer and the shops: which comes first?

TEACHING EXPERIENCES

Many schools organize price comparison exercises and outings to shopping centres. At Oadby Manor School the first and second years visited the local Woolco and had to find answers to questions on price comparisons, store layout and the range of goods. They also chose the product they would most like to buy and had to justify their choice. Most selected a high fashion item much favoured by their age group at the time, complained about its poor quality and price, but nevertheless wanted it because 'it's in fashion'. They later discussed these points in class.

At Swakeleys School the geography fourth years surveyed the local shopping centre, identified shops selling anoraks, noted the price range and interviewed shoppers on why they bought them, finding it was as a casual coat rather than for rugged outdoor activities. In fabric science they examined the fabrics used, and devised tests for showing wear, water resistance, etc.

Bredbury School fourth years took Stockport market as their subject. They mapped the layout of stalls and the goods they sold, surveyed stallholders to find out how far they came and surveyed customers to find what they liked about the market (then under threat of demolition). One group investigated the history of the market from Roman times, and another photographed their activities. The results were sent to the local authority, which had been appealing for local views on the future of the market.

Resources

How to Deal with Doorstep Salesmen, Office of Fair Trading. Free leaflet from Citizens' Advice Bureaux and Consumer Advice Centres.
Shopping at Home, Direct Sales and Service Association, 47 Windsor Road, Slough, Berks, SL1 2EE. Free leaflet.
Shopping Sense, G.M. MacDonald (Forbes Publications, 1975). Factual textbook on the science of shopping. (0 901 762 21 0)

6 Money

Having dealt with where the money goes – in shopping as well as in taxes as an indirect form of payment – the next question is where it comes from, because none of the activities outlined in the previous chapter is possible without money.

In the main it comes from earnings, and also from pensions, state benefits and investments. Schoolchildren however have their own viewpoint on acquiring money, as well as on spending it, and this can be the start when considering money management with them. Moreover, for adult education, pre-retirement and higher education students, the amount of money teenagers and even small children have to spend and what they spend it on are good starting points for discussion. Even higher education students, themselves not long out of school, will eagerly discuss the scandalously high earnings of schoolchildren only a few years younger than themselves, and this can be a useful way of opening discussions about earnings and money among people otherwise reluctant to discuss them.

TEENAGE JOBS

Despite laws restricting the age and number of hours school-age children can work, from around eleven or so many will be trying to find local part-time jobs to supplement or replace the pocket money their parents usually give them. From around thirteen they will be looking for fairly regular part-time employment – as shelf-fillers, delivering newspapers, serving in shops, cleaning up in hairdressers, working in hotels and cafés, washing dishes, serving at tables, working on market stalls, washing cars, caddying at a golf course, gardening, odd jobs. With a tight labour situation it is less easy for them to get jobs than it once was, yet they can nevertheless often find work. Discussion in any class will reveal a wide range of jobs, and an acute awareness of how much work each demands and what they get for it. The money these jobs bring is very highly prized because of the independence and taste of adult life it makes possible.

POCKET MONEY

Pocket money depends on age, sex, geographical location and socio-economic group, as well as on parental attitudes. Several market research surveys, notably by Carrick James, McCann Erickson and Walls Ice Cream, have shown that Scottish boys in the lowest socio-economic groups do best and girls in the south-east from the more affluent income groups do worst – which Scots attribute to the favouritism shown by Scottish mothers to their sons, and southerners attribute to the amount of extras parents in the south-east are expected to pay for. Discussions in class reveal many of these attitudes.

Many children also get lump sums as birthday and Christmas presents from grandparents and relatives living some distance away, who would rather give money than pay postage for something the child might not like. Even where children do not get regular pocket money, they do not appear to go short, but report that their parents give them money when they want it, as often as every day. Even in low-income families the children are the last to feel the pinch; parents may delay paying rent or fuel bills but their children will not go short.

Discussion on these points, which children find of absorbing interest, can lead on to the question of whether their earnings and/or pocket money cover their entire expenditure, and of course they do not: their parents pay for most basics and more besides. However these discussions, including an analysis of what parents do provide, lead into discussions of money management in adult life.

METHODS OF PAYMENT

As well as many ways to shop, there are also many ways to pay. The way you pay affects the price, and may thus also affect where you shop.

Cash is the most obvious method. However, increasingly there are alternatives, most of which cost more but may be more convenient.

Paying by *cheque* costs more than cash because the bank makes a charge to your account, depending on how much you keep in it and how many cheques you draw. In return you have the convenience of your money stored safely and the larger sums transferred to enterprises you wish to pay – shops, electricity board, landlord, etc.

You can also pay by a range of credit transactions, for all of which you pay interest: a *bank loan* for a specific item, such as a car or home improvement, or a *hire purchase* agreement for a particular item. You might also have a *bank overdraft* for unspecified expenditure up to an agreed amount, and you might pay bills out of that. A *mortgage* is another form of loan on which interest is paid.

Credit cards, such as Access, can be used to pay for some item. The loan is interest-free if it is paid within a specified time of a few weeks; otherwise interest is charged. (A *bank card* is issued by certain banks to support cheques drawn by customers on their accounts up to a certain limit. No interest is charged.) Other credit cards, such as American Express, are issued on payment of a yearly subscription; you pay no interest, provided you pay in full when the demand is made. It is another method of deferring payment, perhaps until next month's cheque has been paid.

Some chain stores issue credit cards which work on the same principle as Access: you either pay in full when the bill arrives, or pay in instalments an amount which includes interest. Other stores issue *credit account* cards for customers who make a regular monthly payment by bankers' order and can then spend up to an agreed credit limit – a way of spreading payment.

Another system is *check trading*. Customers buy checks up to an agreed amount and then pay back in weekly sums to a collector who calls at their home. Tallymen offer a similar system of a cash loan paid back on weekly instalments to the tallyman who calls at the door. Money lenders too make arrangements of a lump sum and weekly repayment. Interest rates vary and have been criticized as being unduly high. The National Consumer Council found that some check interest rates were for 45 per cent, and that people with tallyman loans tended not to know the rate of interest, which was high. (See Consumer Credit Act, p. 45).

All these factors are of great concern to consumers, because the method of payment affects the real price. Moreover, although credit arrangements usually mean buying with money you have not yet got, in a period of inflation it makes sense to do that and to defer payment even for a few weeks.

There is also a fundamental dilemma. Clever manipulation of credit can lead to a marked improvement in a family's standard of living; foolhardy spending on credit can lead to debt, hardship and possibly even family break-up and the problems that implies. 'Credit' and 'debt' in fact mean the same thing. These are extremely difficult concepts to put across to children, and not always fully perceived by adults. Significantly, much of the consumer education done among prisoners shortly before release is among those completing sentences for debt and credit offences.

SAVING

Having read about the credit systems available, and learnt that deferring payment can be advantageous in an inflationary period, you and the children you teach may well ask 'why save'? Yet the way to take advantage of the existing credit system is to show that you are worthy of it – creditworthy in fact. Thus a bank will give you a credit card, overdraft or bank loan on learning that you can keep within your income and possibly even put some of it in a building society or other form of saving. Those who are unable to do this are likely to be denied the less expensive forms of credit (there being no 'cheap' forms of credit) and find themselves obliged to get credit from money lenders and other expensive sources.

Teenage savings

Interestingly enough, young people save a good deal. Surveys repeatedly show that at eleven a significant proportion will be putting money aside, though at that age they may not have any particular purchase in view. By the time they are fourteen they are saving for a purchase or an event, such as a holiday, and this habit persists through their teens.

It is possible for a child from eleven upwards to have a bank account, at the discretion of the bank manager who relies on his knowledge of the child's parents, their account, and his judgement of the child. It is however not at all common. Children are more likely to save through National Savings or the Trustee Savings Bank, especially where there is a school bank or there was one in their primary school. Post office accounts are also popular: the money can be easily deposited and withdrawn. At eighteen teenagers can of course open their own bank accounts.

Sometimes children are encouraged to put money in a building society account, from which they cannot draw it until they are eighteen; this again appears to be relatively unusual. Most commonly – and this comes out in class discussions – they trust an adult to look after the money for them. Nevertheless, early experiences of money-handling institutions, like the Post Office, are valuable and should be encouraged, since they will undoubtedly be needed in adult life, if not before. Many of the problems encountered by students in higher education, about which they seek counselling, are caused by their inability to handle their money.

TEACHING EXPERIENCES

School banks are of course a teaching experience in themselves, especially for the child of middle-school age. However any teaching to do with money and methods of payment becomes closely related to particular products and methods of shopping, or decisions about major outgoings, like the choice of housing and paying for it.

A parentcraft teacher got her CSE class to choose the equipment for a first baby from the catalogue of a well-known baby store; this is obviously an emotional experience in any family's life and they chose with enthusiasm. The bill totalled several hundred pounds, though the maternity grant was only £25. The class then compared prices in high street shops, and finally reduced the total still further by calculating how much could be saved by borrowing equipment from relatives: an exercise in budgeting and financial priorities and also in recognizing the special vulnerability of a situation which could lead to heavy expenditure.

Other teachers use travel brochures which children read with enthusiasm and then select their favoured holiday: the rest of the teaching is about how to pay for it. A good deal of careers teaching is based on similar 'goals/payment' principles.

Resources

Money Which? Published quarterly by the Consumers' Association as an adjunct to *Which?* (see p. 55). (Special rates for bulk orders of back numbers by schools.)
Why the Poor Pay More, ed. Frances Williams (see p. 21).
Budgeting: the Guide to the Art of Making Ends Meet, Birmingham Settlement Money Advice Centre. 318 Summer Lane, B19 3RL. Practical advice.
Budgeting for Marriage, National Savings Committee. Poster and teachers' notes.
Money. One of a series produced by the BBC and the National Consumer Council. Deals with budgeting, savings, credit.

About Instalment Credit, free leaflet from Finance Houses Association, 14 Queen Anne's Gate, London, SW1H 9AG. Explains hire purchase.

The Intelligent Use of Consumer Credit, Consumer Credit Association of the United Kingdom, 192A Nantwich Road, Crewe, Cheshire, CW2 6BP. Simple explanation of different forms of credit, though not updated to include the Consumer Credit Act (pp. 45).

Banks produce explanatory booklets for customers which teachers may find useful for their own information and for older pupils: Public Relations Department, Lloyds Bank, PO Box 215, 71 Lombard Street, London EC3P 3BS; Public Relations and Advertising Department, Midland Bank, Griffin House, PO Box 2, 41 Silver Street Head, Sheffield S1 3GG; Advertising and Publicity Department, National Westminster Bank, King's Cross House, 200 Pentonville Road, London N1 9HL; Advertising Department, Barclays Bank, Juxon House, 94 St Paul's Churchyard, London EC4M 8EH, who also have a good poster on the progress of a cheque. The Bank Education Service, 10 Lombard Street, London EC3V 9AT, have an extensive series of free booklets, mainly for A level students or as information for teachers.

Money and Society, Money and You and *Life Assurance and You*: teaching kits. Life Offices Association and Associated Scottish Life Offices Information Centre, 60 Cheapside, London EC2V 6AX, who also produce a free booklet, *Saving and Spending*.

Stop and Think. Office of Fair Trading leaflet on buyers' and sellers' rights on credit transactions, deposits, etc. Free from Citizens' Advice Bureaux and Consumer Advice Centres.

7 Consumer law

A legal framework has developed in most countries around the transactions between producers, traders and consumers. Throughout history there has been some tension in their relationships, to the extent that some form of protection for shoppers against dishonest suppliers has been necessary. As life has become more complicated, and the chain of responsibility from manufacturer to consumer, via importer, wholesaler, and retailer more extended, so consumer law has had to cover this relationship in more detail.

There are three basic principles underlying consumer law in the United Kingdom. First, there is a contract between buyer and seller. Every time you buy a paper or a chocolate bar, or get on a bus, there is a contract between you as the consumer, and the provider of the goods or service. Therefore if anything goes wrong there is a solution in law, although it is unlikely you will actually go to court. Secondly, whatever you are going to buy has to be accurately described: size, amount, colour, etc. Thirdly, it must be safe.

Thus the purchases made on impulse or to fulfil a basic need like hunger or cold come down to these prosaic, legal conditions. If for some reason they are not fulfilled, there is a system of complaint and redress in England and Wales (described more fully in chapter 8) which applies with slight variations to Scotland and Northern Ireland as well.

CIVIL LAW

There is a distinction between *civil law*, where the individual has to take action himself, because he is regarded as being the only person affected, and *criminal law*, where the community as a whole might be affected and the local authority officers therefore act for us all.

As far as consumers are concerned, the major civil laws are the *Sale of Goods Act 1979* which incorporates the 1873 Act and the *Supply of Goods (Implied Terms) Act 1973*. Under these laws, goods must be 'fit for the purpose for which they are intended', i.e. a washing machine must function as a washing machine, or a pair of shoes must be wearable and usable as shoes.

If goods are not 'fit' the retailer (not the manufacturer) must 'repair, or replace' them. In most cases the retailer is prepared to do one or the other, especially in view of the pressure applied in recent years by consumer agencies and the media. However, in cases of difficulty, the consumer in England and Wales can take the case to the County Court himself, without employing a solicitor, under the simplified Small Claims rules. (Regrettably the two experiments in small claims courts on American lines, the Small Claims Arbitration Scheme in Manchester and the London Small Claims Court for the rest of England and Wales have had to close through lack of finance.)

In Scotland the consumer can take the case to the Sheriff Court under the Summary Cause if less than £500 is involved; in Northern Ireland he is more likely to have to employ a solicitor.

The *Unfair Contract Terms Act 1977*, also a civil law, bans the small print exclusion clauses by which organizations – perhaps a car park operator or dry cleaner – attempt to deny responsibility for damage to goods in their care.

CRIMINAL LAW

These are acts passed to protect the community as a whole, and there are a good many, most of them enforced on behalf of the community by trading standards, consumer protection or environmental health officers employed by the local authority.

The *Food and Drugs Act 1955* requires that food shall be fit to eat and wholesome, and 'of the nature, quality and substance demanded'. Thus the manufacturers whose tin of peas contained a large green caterpillar were found guilty, since you would not normally expect to find such a thing in a tin of peas. The Act is reinforced by a wide range of regulations covering many kinds of food such as sausages, meat pies, condensed milk, fish paste, orange squash, etc. which must conform to certain compositional standards – e.g. pork sausages must contain 85 per cent pig meat.

The Act is also supported by the *Food Hygiene (General) Regulations 1968*, which require that food shall be manufactured and prepared and sold in clean and hygienic conditions. These are the Regulations invoked when environmental health officers find evidence of 'gross contamination by vermin' in food shops, or where a pair of trousers was found in the oven meant for warming pies.

The *Labelling of Food Regulations 1970* is also part of the Food and Drugs Act. It means that processed and packaged food, which is more and more the way we buy food nowadays, is about the best labelled of any product you are likely to buy. The requirements of the Regulations are a good pointer to what information other products ought to carry but do not. For example, the product must have a name – and not one which is just an adman's dream, but something which actually tells you what the product is. Thus Coffeemate is also described on the label as 'dried glucose syrup and vegetable fat', which is its technical name. (The exceptions are products which can claim the thirty-year rule, in that if they were in existence thirty years before 1970, they need not use a descriptive name as well as the trade name. Examples are Oxo, Horlicks, and Mars bars.)

The product must also have on it the name and address of the organization responsible for it: i.e. the manufacturer, retailer or importer. The ingredients must be listed in order of quantity, including additives, and the product's name must reflect those ingredients. Thus 'curry with rice and beef' has least beef and most rice. The tin of peas with the large green caterpillar would in fact not have contravened the Food and Drugs Act if it had been labelled 'tinned peas with added caterpillar' although every tin would then have had to contain a caterpillar.

Special claims must be quantified: e.g. vitamin content or low calorific value; no claims can be made that food is 'slimming'. Any claims of that kind must be associated with a rider such as 'only works as part of a calorie-controlled diet'.

The *Weights and Measures Act 1963* requires that products sold by length, weight, volume or number (like fabric, packaged food, liquids and eggs) shall declare that information on the product. Certain products like jam, flour, sugar, fats, dried pulses, etc. must be packed in what are called 'prescribed quantities': i.e. a range of quantities which are generally a multiple of the base weight. In that way a shopper can compare the price of different teas, for example, which is a considerable help. Consumer pressure often focuses on trying to get this list of prescribed quantities extended, for instance to biscuits, which have a wide range of weights. Originally the Act required all this information to be given in imperial measures; gradually this has been amended to metric measures.

The *Trade Descriptions Act 1968* requires that oral, written or visual descriptions of products and services shall be accurate, and shall not mislead 'recklessly' or 'to a material degree'. Second-hand cars often feature in contraventions of this Act: for example when an odometer has been turned back so that the car's mileage looks lower than it is. Because the mileage is part of the car's 'trade description', this is an offence under that act. Similarly, the hotel described in the brochure as 'only five minutes' walk from the beach': if you can only reach the beach in five minutes by clambering down the cliff face, as has been the case, and the journey by road actually takes twenty minutes, once again there has been an offence under the Act. But the misleading description has to be about a physical, verifiable feature; claims like 'the holiday of a lifetime' or 'lovelier than ever before' are expected to be taken with a pinch of salt. They cannot be quantified and are not part of the 'trade description'. Nevertheless a 'trade description' can be given

orally by a shop assistant, in writing in a leaflet or advertise-
ment, or visually, as when the picture of the contents suggests
that you get more than you actually do.

The *Trade Descriptions Act 1972* deals with the country of
origin as part of the trade description: when for example an
imported item looks as though it was made in the United
Kingdom (perhaps a teapot decorated with a Union Jack, or a
shirt labelled with a British trade mark), the country of origin
must be declared on the label.

The *Consumer Protection Acts 1961 and 1971* laid down that
products be safe. They operated through Regulations covering
particular groups of products. Thus there are the Toy Safety
Regulations, the Electric Blanket Regulations, the Heating
Appliance Regulations, and others covering the stability of cot
stands, fire guards, pencils, children's outer garments
fastened by drawn cord, such as anoraks, and several more.
The Regulations specify standards for these products, so that,
for example, the paint on children's toys must not contain lead
and the eyes of soft toys must be securely anchored and not on
spikes; girls' nightdresses must be of flame-proof fabric; paraf-
fin heaters must be of a design which will not tip over.
Over the years it became clearer that this was not enough;
more products were outside the regulations than were
included within them. There was for example the case of a
sweet made to look like a baby's dummy but designed in such
a way that it might have choked a small baby. The prosecution
under the Toy Safety Regulations failed because the importers'
defence was that it was a sweet and not a toy, and therefore not
covered by the Regulations. Moreover, another weakness of
the Acts was that a product could be withdrawn in one local
authority area as the result of a prosecution but could continue
to be sold elsewhere in the country, although trading
standards departments operate an unofficial information
system to try to avoid this happening. Thus the *Consumer
Safety Act 1978* was passed, which incorporates the Regulations under the old Consumer Protection Acts. It requires that

all products shall be safe, and provides for quick action, on a national scale, against any type of consumer product found to be dangerous. For example, when stink bombs which might have been harmful to eyes and the respiratory system were found on sale in joke shops soon after the Act reached the statute book, they were quickly banned and withdrawn throughout the country, which would not have been possible under the earlier Acts.

The *Fair Trading Act 1973* is an important piece of consumer legislation with wide powers. It set up the office of Director General of Fair Trading, with the responsibility of looking after consumers' health, safety and economic interests. This is partly done by a very active programme of consumer information, so that consumers know their rights, and by setting up codes of practice with industries where consumer difficulties are well known – examples are the codes relating to the sale and repair of footwear, the servicing and repair of electrical appliances, the sale, servicing and repair of second-hand cars, package tour holidays, mail order transactions, funeral charges, laundering and dry cleaning, and a number of others.

The Act also gives power to refer companies for investigation by the Monopolies and Mergers Commission and by the Restrictive Practices Court, both of which try to increase the competitiveness of business by preventing policies contrary to consumers' interests, such as price fixing, where the consumer is not paying the true price, and dominance of a market by heavy expenditure on advertising to such an extent that competition is excluded and consumers pay for the advertising in the high price of the product.

Another aspect of the Fair Trading Act is that the Director General can, if a company persists in breaking consumer laws, demand an undertaking from the company and the directors personally that they will do so no longer. Examples have been a shop selling jeans which refused to refund money or replace faulty goods, a chain of cafés and restaurants which had been prosecuted many times for dirty premises, and a hi fi mail order company which took money, did not send goods in return, and would not return money. The Director General also investigates practices thought to be against the consumers' interests in terms of health, safety, and economic interests, such as prices declared exclusive of VAT, and bargain offers publicized in such a way as to look much cheaper than they are. The Fair Trading Act excludes the nationalized industries from these investigations; more recently the *Competition Act 1980* has made it possible for the Director General to investigate nationalized industries and to refer them to the Monopolies and Mergers Commission for investigation into possible abuses of their monopoly positions.

He is responsible for the *Consumer Credit Act 1974*. Any organization offering loans, advice on loans or on payment of debts, or information about creditors, must be licensed by the Director General. This includes banks, accountants, mortgage brokers, building societies, as well as consumer and other advice agencies who give debt advice free. It also includes money lenders and tallymen. Any loan or agreement arranged by a non-licensed body is void.

Under the Act, credit cannot be refused on grounds of race or sex. The true rate of interest over a year must be declared and not just the interest by the month, and consumers must be told the price of the goods including interest payments as well as the period of time over which payment is required.

When people apply for a loan, many companies check with a credit reference agency to see whether they are habitual bad debtors. Mistakes have been known to occur, as when an agency might 'black' all the people in a block of flats because of one bad debtor living there. Under the Consumer Credit Act anyone who thinks that wrong information is being held about him or her, can, for a small fee, see the records, and get them put right.

The *Prices Acts 1974 and 1975* have a number of provisions which are gradually being brought into force, such as the display of the price of some goods at point of sale, and the unit price, (i.e., the price per unit of weight or volume), which must be declared on prepacked cheese, meat and a few other products.

There are a number of other Acts passed to deal with particular conditions. The *Trading Stamps Act 1964* means that trading stamps have a face value and can be exchanged for cash. The *Unsolicited Goods and Services Act 1971* was introduced to stop the practice of sending goods people had not asked for and then demanding payment. Under the Act, if you do not want the goods you must inform the company within thirty days, and keep them in a clean and undamaged condition. If after six months the company have not collected them, the goods are yours.

This is by no means a complete list of consumer laws; there are many others which affect consumers, like the *Clean Air Acts*, the *Electricity Acts*, the *Gas Acts* and many more. But this is the group usually regarded as having been passed specifically to protect consumers.

Added to them are the directives agreed by the European Community, which we incorporate in our laws as part of our obligations in accepting membership. Several are intended as consumer protection measures and are either incorporated in our acts as regulations, or in acts of their own. Thus the *Fibre Content Regulations* are part of the *European Communities Act*; they oblige manufacturers to label garments with the names of the main fibres and their proportions. The *Cosmetic Safety Regulations* were introduced under the Consumer Protection Acts as the result of a directive. They oblige manufacturers to state the presence in cosmetics and toiletries of known irritants or allergens – a first step toward getting ingredient labelling for cosmetics and toiletries.

This is part of the EEC harmonization programme, by which products cannot be prevented from passing freely between the countries of the Community by any national laws or standards which might exclude them. That was the original intention of forming the Community – to set up a very large free market and to remove what are called 'barriers to trade'. However the European Commission has since adopted a commitment to improving the quality of life and the environment for the people living within it, and thus has a consumer programme aimed at providing consumers across the Community with the same level of consumer information, protection, safety standards, economic safeguards, redress and consumer education. To this end the Commission tries to 'harmonize' the laws and practices of all the member countries to arrive at a universally accepted directive – not an easy or quick matter. The results are 'optional' or 'obligatory' directives, though the UK ignores this distinction and incorporates them all into our law either as regulations if they are obligatory directives, or as Acts of their own if the directives are optional.

TEACHING EXPERIENCES

An exhibition can be organized around the theme of consumer law in operation. Examples include labels from food, clothing and toiletries, as well as advertisements making specific claims for products, travel brochures, and newspaper cuttings on prosecutions over consumer laws. Thus the exhibition can focus on one Act, like the Trade Descriptions Act, or on consumer law in general.

One teacher incorporated consumer choice, consumer law and consumer redress in one lesson by showing her class fashion pictures of trousers; they discussed which they preferred, and acted buying them. Then they acted taking them back because of a complaint, and taped the transactions. Interestingly, those with least confidence and lowest ability became the most aggressive and insisted most forcibly on their rights.

Resources

Consumer News, Information Division, Consumer Affairs Division, Department of Trade, 1 Victoria Street, London SW1H 0ET. Free newsletter, 6 times a year. Up-to-date information about developments and changes in consumer law and organisations, with a regular section on consumer education.

Euroforum, Directorate-General of Information, Commission of the European Communities, 200 Rue de la Loi, B-1049, Brussels, Belgium. Free newsletter, 11 times a year. Events and proposals within the EEC for consumer affairs, the environment, social and economic issues.

Consumer Laws

The Consumer, Society and the Law, Gordon Borrie and Aubrey L. Diamond (Penguin, 1977). Invaluable guide, with many useful cases as examples which could be used in class work. (0 14 02.0647 7)

Suzie and the supershopper, Heinemann and Inner London Education Authority (1974). Teaching kit on the Sale of Goods Act. (0 435 422324)

Dog Days. Amusing cartoon slide/tape kit by the Office of Fair Trading on shopping and the Sale of Goods Act, featuring O'Shaunessy the dog, and *Further Adventures of O'Shaunessy*, on the Trade Descriptions Act. Both from Central Film Library, Government Buildings, Bromyard Avenue, London W3 7JB.

Small Claims in the County Court, Citizens' Advice Bureaux and Consumer Advice Centres. Free explanatory booklet.

How to Sue in the County Courts, Consumers' Association.

Simple Justice: A Consumer View of Small Claims Procedures in England and Wales. National Consumer Council and Welsh Consumer Council Report (1979). (0 905653 23 8)

Alice in Label Land. Attractive cartoon film on the Labelling of Food Regulations. Central Film Library (see above).

Consumers: Know Your Rights, John Harries (Oyez, 1978). Advice on wide range of problems, including fireworks, hiring goods, contracts with children. (0 85120 346 6)

Fair Deal on Credit: A Brief Guide to the Consumer Credit Act, How to Put Things Right (England and Wales), *Dear Shopper in Northern Ireland, Dear Shopper in Scotland*, Office of Fair Trading. Leaflets on consumer rights and redress. Free from Citizens' Advice Bureaux and Consumer Advice Centres.

Codes of Practice

The Office of Fair Trading produces a series of attractive and informative leaflets on the Codes of Practice introduced under the Fair Trading Act. Titles include: *Package Holidays, Package Holidays Abroad, Furniture, Shoes, Funerals, Electrical Goods, Launderers and Dry Cleaners* and *Cars*. Free from Citizens' Advice Bureaux and Consumer Advice Centres.

8 Consumer protection and consumer organizations

The structure of consumer protection, information and representation in the United Kingdom is one of organizations which have developed out of the consumer laws described in chapter 7. The system operates on several levels, almost as a series of filters – central government, local government and independent consumer organizations, all with different functions. It may seem complex, largely for historical reasons, but it is important to understand who does what and how each one is financed. Not all can deal with complaints from the public, which are in fact a relatively small part of consumer affairs. Far greater is the effort put into information, pressure group activities, legislation and monitoring functions.

GOVERNMENT DEPARTMENTS

As governments have changed in the seventies, so too has the official attitude to consumer affairs. This was first given official recognition in 1972 under the Conservative Administration, when the Department of Trade and Consumer Affairs was formed, and given a Minister of Cabinet rank. The 1974 Labour Government set up the Department of Prices and Consumer Protection, also with its own Secretary of State in the Cabinet. With the Conservative return to office in 1979, consumer affairs lost its own department, and became the Consumer Affairs Division of the Department of Trade, with a junior Minister responsible for it. (Certain functions are undertaken by the Welsh Office, the Scottish Development Department, and the Northern Ireland Department of Commerce.)

The Consumer Affairs Division of the Department of Trade, 1

Victoria Street, London SW1H 0ET, deals with prices, trading practices as they affect the consumer (e.g. rates charges by *bureaux de change*, the flammability of substances used in furniture), grants to consumer bodies, including the National Consumer Council and the nationalized industry consumer councils, competition policy, weights and measures, consumer safety, consumer advice and much more, affecting consumers across a broad spectrum of activities, including relations with the European Commission over harmonization of consumer laws (see pp. 46–7).

The Consumer Safety Unit in particular has led the world in setting up the accident surveillance scheme with hospitals to collate and analyse the causes of accidents in the home, in order to identify the age groups at risk, practices that cause accidents, and the products involved. It reports regularly on the results, and also on deaths due to the use of electricity in the home (see p. 64).

Several other government departments also have consumer responsibilities. The *Ministry of Agriculture, Fisheries and Food*, Whitehall Place, London SW1A 2HH, deals with food standards, food hygiene, supplies of food, some prices such as milk, and other matters relating to the way the country is fed and the standard of its diet. It has a number of committees, such as the Food Additives and Contaminants Committee, dealing with such questions as the level of lead in food and the safety of colouring matters in food; the Food Standards Committee looks at questions such as nutritional labelling, whether water content should be labelled, and many similar issues; other committees have reported on the date-marking of food, the quality of potatoes, and much else. All these committees have consumer representatives, scientific experts and representatives of retailers and manufacturers. The Ministry of Agriculture is also directly concerned with the European Commission over such questions as the Common Agricultural Policy, subsidies to farmers, and food surpluses.

The *Department of Health and Social Security*, Alexander Fleming House, Elephant and Castle, London SE1 6BY has a range of activities affecting consumers in relation to the operation of the National Health Service and the provisions of the state system of benefits.

The *Department of the Environment*, 2 Marsham Street, London SW1P 3EB is involved with matters such as local authority housing, housing associations and building societies, as well as environmental matters like the conservation of buildings, measures to preserve the beauty of the landscape and clean air.

The *Department of Trade*, apart from consumer affairs, is also concerned with the operation of airlines and airports, the tourist and holiday industry and the insurance industry, all of which affect consumers.

The *Department of Energy*, Thames House South, Millbank, London SW1P 4QJ deals with the way the coal, gas and electricity industries fulfil their obligations to consumers, including the profits they make and such far-reaching decisions as the building of nuclear coal-fired power stations which affect consumers through the price and supply of electricity. It has an Energy Conservation Division to encourage energy saving among commerce, industry, and consumers.

The *Department of Transport*, 2 Marsham Street, London SW1P 3EB has similar responsibility for British Rail, its relations with its users and its level of profitability, for the road transport system and the building and provision of motorways.

These are just a few of the ways some government departments have an impact on consumers' lives: there is in fact no government department without a consumer responsibility of some kind or another. However, in the United Kingdom government departments have a supervisory function as to how laws are carried out, and they are sometimes involved with initiating them, but the laws themselves are administered by local authority departments, whose work in relation to consumers is looked at in more detail on pp. 53–5.

A number of government-financed agencies have been set up to protect and represent consumers' interests. The *Office of Fair Trading*, Field House, Breams Buildings, London EC4A 1PR was established in 1973 when the office of Director General of Fair Trading was created by the Fair Trading Act (see pp. 44–5).

The *National Consumer Council*, 18 Queen Anne's Gate, London SW1H 9AA had a predecessor in the old Consumer Council set up in 1963 and closed down in 1971 by the incoming Conservative Government, who were much criticized for this economy measure. Subsequently, and with another change of government, the *National Consumer Council* was set up in 1975 with the *Scottish Consumer Council*, 4 Somerset Place, Glasgow G3 7JT, the *Welsh Consumer Council*, 8 St Andrew's Place, Cardiff CF1 3BE, and the *Northern Ireland Consumer Council*, 176 Newtownbreda Road, Belfast BT8 4QS. Their brief is to co-ordinate the work of the consumer organizations, to look after consumers' interests, particularly those on low incomes, to protect consumers' interests during the change-over to metrication, and to improve consumer representation, particularly in the European Community. They act as pressure groups where consumers are placed in an inequitable position, and they give wide publicity to these situations.

The *Metrication Board*, Millbank Tower, London SW1P 4QU, was set up after the decision to change to metric measures, in line with the Continent and major world markets. Its function was to prepare the way for metrication in the retail trade, in industry, and among consumers, including schoolchildren. It operated mainly by disseminating information, and had no powers to enforce metrication. It was closed down early in 1980, partly as an economy measure, and partly because the government of the day felt its work was almost over, since it was decided to make metrication a voluntary and not an obligatory measure.

The *British Standards Institution*, 2 Park Street, London W1A 2BS is funded partly by industry, partly by the sales of its publications and partly by government. It sets standards for many thousands of industrial products, like street lighting columns and steel sections, but also many consumer products. Standards are related to particular specifications, such as dimensions, composition, safety, etc. and the BS number can be used on products which conform to the standard.

Consumer standards are establishing with the co-operation of the *Consumer Standards Advisory Committee*, which represents the women's and consumer organizations, and has a secretariat within BSI. BSI plays an active role in consumer education and in publicizing the need for standards and their value to consumers.

The BS Kitemark is awarded to companies who apply for a licence to use it and whose products conform to a Standard. They must agree to spot checks within the factory by BSI inspectors. In agreement with the *British Electrotechnical Approvals Board* (BEAB, Mark House, The Green, 9–10 Queen's Road, Hersham, Walton-on-Thames KT12 5NA), electrical appliances sold in the UK are manufactured to British Standards in respect of safety and carry the BEAB/BSI safety symbol which incorporates the kitemark. Certain other appliances such as gas cookers also carry a British Standards safety mark.

LOCAL AUTHORITIES

Local government departments are responsible for enforcing consumer protection laws within their own areas. This means that they have very considerable experience of local trading conditions, which they channel to the relevant government departments and to the Office of Fair Trading — a flow of information which is particularly important when a change in the law seems necessary because of a particular trading practice or a product which is causing difficulties. They can be found through the local telephone directory.

Environmental Health Departments of local authorities deal with contraventions of the Food and Drugs Act and its Regulations (see pp. 40–2); officers inspect premises where food is made or sold and follow up complaints from the public. They are also responsible for a wide range of legislation covering air and noise pollution, housing, conditions in abattoirs and other matters relating to public health.

Trading Standards Departments, sometimes called consumer protection departments, deal with the Weights and Measures Act, the Trade Descriptions Acts, consumer safety legislation, the Consumer Credit Act and a great deal of other legislation (see pp. 42–5). For example, under the Weights and Measures Act, they check the accuracy of petrol pumps and air pressure equipment on filling station forecourts, they check the licences of traders offering credit, they look out for dangerous toys, prices displayed in a misleading way, or signs in shops which deprive shoppers of their legal rights (such as 'no exchanges: credit notes only'). Like the environmental health officers, they deal with many complaints from the public.

Both departments can recommend to their legal departments that companies or trades be prosecuted under the consumer acts, but in practice they try to avoid it in favour of first trying to persuade the companies to change their practices or withdraw whatever product is contravening the law. However if a company persists in breaking or defying the law, it can be prosecuted.

Consumer Advice Centres were set up with government grants for the first year, on the understanding that thereafter they would be funded by the local authority. Thus with changes of political control at local elections, some have been closed and others opened. They are usually part of the consumer protection or trading standards department, and situated in high streets where people can walk in with their complaints and enquiries. Some also operate mobile complaints centres. Consumer Advice Centres are staffed by trained advisers who are expert in local conditions and contract law. Where they have space, they offer pre-shopping advice as well, as a significant proportion of enquiries are from people wanting to know about washing machines or cookers. Many of the advisers are active in consumer education with local schools.

Complaints handled by environmental health departments, trading standards and consumer protection departments, and consumer advice centres are fed into the Office of Fair Trading computer (p. 53). The results identify the problem areas where action is especially needed, perhaps in the form of a Code of Practice or a special order under the Fair Trading Act. It also reveals which companies repeatedly break consumer laws and where action may be needed under the Fair Trading Act (see pp. 44–5).

CONSUMER ORGANIZATIONS

A number of organizations came into existence independently of the government to represent consumers either wholly or as part of their other activities. Inflation has made life increasingly difficult for the voluntary consumer organizations, most of which have died off as costs of postage, telephones, travel and printing have risen, and also because so many women, formerly the backbone of voluntary work, have gone back to work and no longer have time to spare.

The *Consumers' Association*, 14 Buckingham Street, London WC2N 6DS, however, is not a voluntary organization but a limited company set up in 1957 to test products and publish the results. By 1979 it had over 650,000 subscribers to the monthly magazine *Which?* and the quarterly magazines *Money Which?*, *Holiday Which?*, *Handyman Which?* and *Motoring Which?* as well as a range of paperbacks on subjects widely related to consumer affairs, like slimming, backache, and getting a divorce. It runs the Advice Centre Servicing Unit to train staff for consumer advice centres (see p. 54); it works with the

Open University on its consumer courses, and has been active in consumer education; it also lobbies and acts as a pressure group on subjects where it thinks the law needs changing.

The publicity the Consumers' Association has achieved over the years is probably the most influential means by which people at large, not necessarily *Which?* subscribers, are alerted to their roles and rights as consumers.

The *National Federation of Consumer Groups*, Office 7, 70–76 Alcester Road South, Birmingham B14 7PT, has around fifty groups at any one time, as well as individual members, associates (other consumer organizations and companies taking an interest in their work) and associate members (schools and clubs). It gets a small grant from the government, but apart from that soldiers on from year to year, relying on voluntary effort. It represents important and highly respected grass roots activity: the groups focus mainly on local conditions, such as the price, amount and quality of local take-away food or the state and siting of local public lavatories, but they also work on national projects, like the extent of overpackaging and whether the Office of Fair Trading codes of practice are working. Certain groups have been very active in consumer education for both adults and schools.

The *National Association of Citizens' Advice Bureaux*, 110 Drury Lane, London WC2B 5SW is the central organization for about 800 Citizens' Advice Bureaux in England and Wales, which have 95 per cent volunteer staff, often with a part-time or full-time paid organizer. Funds come from local government and central government grants. CABx deal with a very wide range of personal difficulties, which can be legal, financial or marital, as well as consumer problems. This wide range of advice is important, because many problems are far from simple but involve several factors. For example a person in financial difficulties is likely to have fuel debts as well as hire purchase debts, and may also have marital problems as well as difficulties with accommodation and employment.

Many of the complaints handled by Citizens' Advice Bureaux are fed into the Office of Fair Trading computer (p. 53).

There are other agencies to which people go for help – welfare rights, legal advice, social services, neighbourhood advice centres – and many of their appeals to these organizations are for consumer advice, e.g. over high fuel bills which they are unable to pay.

Women's organizations, notably the *National Federation of Women's Institutes*, with 400,000 members, the *National Union of Townswomen's Guilds*, with around 160,000 members, the *National Council of Women* (7,000 members), the *National Association of Women's Clubs* and others, become involved with consumer matters because their members are concerned, and because they are asked for their views on particular subjects by the government. They usually channel their views through the Consumer Standards Advisory Committee (p. 53) and the Consumers in the European Community Group (p. 60), as well as communicating their members' reactions directly to the government.

The *Co-operative Union*, Stanford Hall, Loughborough, LE12 5QR, represents some millions of consumers who are Co-op members, and has traditionally been concerned about consumers since the first co-operative opened in Rochdale in 1842. Every year the education branch organizes the National Consumer Project, in which groups of members all over the country discuss topics of consumer interest such as consumers and leisure, and consumers and waste.

They meet annually to continue these discussions with other groups and to propose resolutions which eventually reach the government, official bodies, industry and consumer bodies with requests for answers and action.

NATIONALIZED INDUSTRY CONSUMER COUNCILS

The Post Office, British Rail, and the gas and electricity supply industries are excluded from many of the contractual obligations of consumer legislation, having separate legislation of their own. They are very large monopolies, highly structured, and traditionally have the reputation of being insensitive to the consumer voice, while at the same time playing a large role in consumers' lives and being responsible for a part of their expenditure. Thus nationalized industry consumer councils have been established to look after consumers of these services (and see p. 45 for the Competition Act and the nationalized industries).

When gas and electricity were nationalized in the 1940s into very large, separate monopolies, each area or region, whether gas or electricity, had to set up a consultative council which it was obliged to consult on such matters as price increases. Over the years these councils have increasingly taken up complaints from consumers with the boards; by the 1960s responsibility for these councils was removed from the industries to government – first the Ministry of Power, then the Department of Prices and Consumer Protection, and then the Consumer Affairs Division of the Department of Trade (or the Scottish Development Department and the Northern Ireland Department of Commerce where relevant) – which pays their salaries and grants them funds to operate.

These are the *regional gas consumer councils* and the *area electricity consultative councils*, whose addresses are on the back of the gas and electricity bills and displayed in local gas and electricity showrooms. Each has a small, paid secretariat and an unpaid council of members who represent local interests, including consumer interests. They are appointed by the Secretary of State for Trade. They discuss tariff proposals – usually for price rises put forward by the gas or electricity board – and matters related to the way consumers are treated by the board. Each council also has several district committees, made up of local people appointed by the area council, and dealing with complaints brought to them personally by consumers who get their names and addresses from the local showroom.

There are also national councils. The *National Gas Consumers' Council*, 5th Floor, Estate House, Jermyn Street, London SW1Y

4UL, represents gas consumers in the United Kingdom, and the *Electricity Consumers' Council*, 119 Marylebone Road, London NW1 5PY, represents electricity consumers in England and Wales. The chairmen of the area or regional councils create a link between their own councils and boards by being part-time members of their boards and also members of the national councils. Scottish electricity consumers can approach the *South of Scotland* or the *North of Scotland Electricity Consultative Councils*, North Clyde Street Lane, Edinburgh EH1 3EW, and electricity consumers in Northern Ireland can go to the *Northern Ireland Electricity Consumers' Council*, Stranmillis Embankment, Belfast BT9 5FN.

The *Domestic Coal Consumers' Council*, Gavrelle House, 2 Bunhill Row, London EC1Y 8LL, is unusual in having industry as well as consumer representatives. It has no local councils but close links with the Approved Coal Merchants' Scheme through whose members complaints can be made.

The *Post Office Users' National Council*, Waterloo Bridge House, Waterloo Road, London SE1 8UA, deals with complaints about the postal services and the telephone, as well as acting as a watchdog over prices and the way consumers are treated. There are some local committees and councils for Scotland, Wales and Northern Ireland, but not the national network that exists for electricity and gas.

There are eleven area transport users' consultative committees, including those for Scotland, Wales and Northern Ireland. Their addresses are displayed in British Rail stations. The *Central Transport Consultative Committee*, 3–4 Great Marlborough Street, London W1V 2EA, deals with national matters, while the area committees tend to deal with local matters such as the effect of line closures. None has the right to deal with prices, bus or air services. The *Airline Users' Committee*, Aviation House, 129 Kingsway, London WC2B 6NN, is financed by the Civil Aviation Authority, and there are airport users' consultative committees for British airports, financed by the British Airports Authority.

Apart from those relating to airports and air transport, all the nationalized industry consumer councils are funded by government and the members are appointed by the Secretary of State; they work on the principle that the consumer with a complaint must first go to the industry concerned, and if not satisfied to the relevant consumer body, usually at local level, where s/he can often get more sympathetic treatment. On matters such as price rises most of the nationalized industry consumer councils have the right to be consulted, although this does not mean that their advice is followed. In general they act, with varying degrees of success and enthusiasm, as pressure groups, by bringing problems to light through the media, by protesting to the government and by protests to the industries themselves.

THE EUROPEAN COMMISSION

The prime function of the European Community is to remove barriers to trade within the member states. A far-reaching programme of harmonization of laws has been undertaken (see pp. 46–7).

The *Environment and Consumer Protection Service* of the European Commission, 200 de la Loi, Brussels B-1049, acts as a focus for the consumer impact on directives which seem relevant to consumers, as well as organizing the consumer voice on matters like the Common Agricultural Policy. To find out what consumers think in member countries, the service commissions research, but mainly acts as a secretariat for the *Consumer Consultative Committee* which is made up of representatives from consumer organizations, family organizations (which are very strong on the Continent), the co-operative movement, and trade unions, which are also important in the consumer world in Europe. The service also briefs consumer members of the Economic and Social Committee, members of the European Parliament, and the Commissioners themselves, when directives are being debated.

In the United Kingdom, the consumer voice on these directives and on the Common Agricultural Policy is in most instances co-ordinated by the *Consumers in the European Community Group*, 4th Floor, 29 Queen Anne's Gate, London SW1H 9AA, which was set up and funded by the government to draw on the views of women's and consumer organizations.

CONSUMER REPRESENTATIVES

At this point it is worth considering the role of consumer representatives in this complex structure of consumer protection. Many of these committees and councils need people to represent consumers; increasingly they look for them outside the somewhat narrow world of the consumer organizations, perhaps among housewives, working people, minorities, the handicapped, the elderly, etc. This poses real problems because few housewives with school-age children can get to afternoon meetings in London; working men and women cannot always get time off, and nor can students and school children, increasingly important in the consumer market and almost entirely unrepresented on these bodies.

Finding people willing and able to serve on, for example, the Consumer Standards Advisory Committee, the Consumers in the European Community Group, the Nationalized Industry Consumer Councils, the National Consumer Council, the Consumer Consultative Committee, and many more, presents problems, partly in avoiding appointing the same people over and over again, and partly because once they are consumer representatives they become to some extent specialists and no longer so truly representative of ordinary people. However their role is undoubtedly valuable, and so far no better alternative has emerged.

COMPLAINTS DEPARTMENT

We have still not reached the limits of complaints systems. The vast majority of complaints are taken up with the retailer, which is as it should be. It means that many cases which are really contraventions of environmental health or trading standards law never come to light, and that the real number of complaints is never known, but there is no doubt that for most people this is the simplest and most effective way. Most responsible retailers, faced with the brunt of consumer complaints to the media, and with complaints from their own staff who have to deal with irate customers, set up reasonably efficient complaints systems.

Of course, not everyone complains when there is just cause; surveys show that possibly no more than 2 per cent of customers do so either because they lack confidence, or knowledge, or time, because it is not convenient, or not sufficiently important for them. Some do write to manufacturers; their letters are dealt with by departments often called 'consumer relations', which are part of the public relations department. Quite a number of people are encouraged to write to manufacturers about their products by the guarantees and similar statements on, such things as packets of sweets and washing powder. The more responsible companies see their replies as a chance to create a favourable impression on the consumer, and also to guage reactions to products and policies, as well as the development of consumer pressure. The less responsible either ignore the letters, or reply in terms so evasive or bland as to make the already aggrieved consumer even more irate than before. Thus do many of the lengthy consumer complaints sagas start.

THE MEDIA

Although this section on consumer protection has been left till last, it is in fact an extremely important part of the build-up of consumer pressure. Journalists working on newspapers and magazines, and broadcasters on radio and television are often concerned by the way products are promoted through advertisements in the media, and learn about cases where individuals have had problems they have not been able to handle. Yet, amazingly and in fact unjustly as this easy response should apply to every complaint, such problems are soon solved when a newspaper or programme raises the issue with the shop or the manufacturer. There are also investigative and concerned journalists and broadcasters who take up cases or enquire into particular situations; very often editors and producers become concerned too, realizing that an exposé is good for sales or listening figures (though less good for their reputations with their advertising department). Problems have been spotlighted in the media as a result, and this has been an important source of pressure for change, for example in the law, in encouraging the Office of Fair Trading to set up codes of practice, and for government to increase consumer representation bodies.

Just as important, the media are a channel for information to reach consumers about their rights, about changes in the law, and about abuses. They also act as very active watchdogs in making sure that government departments and politicians do not backslide on their promise to consumers. Thus, though the consumer organizations have relatively small memberships in relation to the whole population, they have a far wider power base than their numbers would suggest through their contacts with the media, whom they use as a channel for spreading consumer information and for hearing about consumer problems and injustices.

TEACHING EXPERIENCES

Exhibitions of newspaper cuttings based on consumer issues, such as the closing of a railway station or an electricity board showroom, are quite common, as are exhibitions of consumer information published in magazines. Some teachers take a class through their own complaints, or the complaint of someone in the class, monitoring all the different stages; others get the children to write to manufacturers for information on a particular point, such as packaging. Apart from giving experience in writing letters, the replies are an interesting study in communication – or non-communication when the reply is a fulsome expression of goodwill but does not answer the question.

A south London teacher organized an exercise in role-playing by providing desk cards with job titles, such as 'manufacturer', 'shop manager', 'consumer adviser' and so forth, and gave the rest of the class complaints to sort out. They acted as troubled consumers, going from desk to desk asking for help and being referred until they got their difficulties dealt with. Apparently these children found this helpful in dealing with their own consumer problems later on.

Resources

The Consumer Jungle, Marion Giordan (Fontana, 1974). Analysis of the circumstances leading to the development of the consumer situation, and the network of laws and organizations set up to deal with it. (0 00 613359 2)
Commentary on Electrical Fatalities in the Home 1976, The Home Accident and Surveillance System: the first twelve months data, and the *Home Accident Surveillance System: analysis of domestic accidents to children.*
Free from the Information Division, Department of Trade (p. 49), who will also supply the *Dangers and Disasters* teaching kit produced by British Standards Institution, Consumers' Association and the Department of Trade.
Food Facts. Statistics on food consumption, produced approximately six times a year by the Ministry of Agriculture (p. 50). Free to school libraries.
Get Smart, Fair Deal, and *The Work of the Office of Fair Trading.* Free booklets produced by the Office of Fair Trading (p. 52).
Annual Report (A5 sae), leaflets and publications list. National Consumer Council (p. 52).
Consumers and the Nationalised Industries, National Consumer Council (1976) (0 11 880236 4)
The *Scottish Consumer Council* (p. 52) and the *Welsh Consumer Council* (p. 52) also produce reports.

British Standards Institution (pp. 52–3) has a free list of its consumer education materials, which include films and teaching packs. Free leaflets include *Your Questions Answered about British Standards, Just How many Risks have You Bought Lately, What Every Mum and Dad Should Know* as well as *BSI Consumer Report,* a free newsletter on British Standards.

Mark of Safety. Free leaflet about the BEAB symbol (p. 00) and the work of the board.

The EHO. Free leaflet on the work of the environmental health officer, from the Environmental Health Officers' Association, 19 Grosvenor Place, London SW1X 7HU.

Consumer Safety and the Trading Standards Officer, and *The Trading Standards/Consumer Protection Service*. Free leaflets. Institute of Trading Standards Administration, Estate House, 319D London Road, Hadleigh, Benfleet, Essex SS7 2BN.

A number of consumer advice centres, for example Harlow, produce their own consumer leaflets. Lambeth Consumer Services produce *It's A Comic* for Lambeth middle-school children: the first was on weights and measures and the second on electricity. Croydon Consumer Services have produced an audio-visual presentation on shopping problems and redress, featuring school age children. Tyne and Wear Consumer Services also produce worksheets and other teaching materials. These resources are only available to local schools, and it is worth finding out what is happening in your area.

Which?, published monthly by Consumers' Association (pp. 55–6), is essential reading for all teachers of consumer education and related subjects. Issues include booklists of other publications, such as *The Buyer's Right*, a *Which?* guide for consumers.

Paper Bags, an information pack, is produced by the National Federation of Consumer Groups (p. 56) for schools. Single copies free.

Citizens' Advice Bureau (free cartoon leaflet aimed at teenagers) and *The Citizens' Advice Bureau Service*. National Association of Citizens' Advice Bureaux (p. 56).

Help! (advice on safety, complaints, and how to calculate the cost of consumption), free from the National Gas Consumers' Council (p. 58).

Problems with Electricity (cartoon leaflet suitable for schools), *Consumers and Electricity* (leaflet), *Annual Report*, and *Teachers' Resource List on Electricity, Consumers and Conservation*. Electricity Consumers' Council (p. 58). A4 sae for extensive list of materials produced by industry, government, pressure groups and educational publishers.

Consumers of Power: Measuring and Improving the Performance of the London Electricity Board, Charles Medawar (Social Audit Ltd, 1980). Lively and penetrating investigation into the performance and activities of one of the electricity boards, commissioned by the London Electricity Consultative Council and the Electricity Consumers' Council.

An Important Message to All Domestic Solid Fuel Users. Free 'how to complain' leaflet from Domestic Coal Consumers' Council (p. 59).

Annual Report and *What is POUNC?* (leaflet). Free from the Post Office Users' National Council (p. 59).

How to Handle Customer Complaints, Chris Moore (Gower Press, 1976). Industry's view on how to handle consumers.

9 The consumer and the environment

A distasteful aspect of the consumer society is the waste it creates. This is something we are increasingly aware of and want to find solutions for, especially as shortages make it clear that western European society no longer has first call on the rest of the world for resources, and moreover that those resources, on which our consumer society depends, are running out.

In 1977 the population of the European Community created 95m tonnes of waste, in the form of waste paper, packaging, vegetable waste, and so forth, of which 80% was household waste. This wasteful side of the consumer society is something many find ethically unacceptable, and, to their credit, many of them are children and young people.

But waste is not quite the right word for materials we throw away. It is waste when we have finished with it, but until then it was packaging, newspaper, a pair of jeans, a car, or an apple core. Until these objects became waste products they all had an apparent justification and now they have none. We are increasingly realizing that their history must not stop there: there is an urgent need for recycling and further use of materials, as well as for conservation of materials, and avoidance of waste in the first place.

PACKAGING

The element of waste people focus on is usually packaging, although there are many other things, like used cars, old engine oil, broken electrical appliances, old bedsteads and toys, old clothes, and old magazines and newspapers. They all represent something which now apparently has no function (though this need not be so and is discussed in more detail on pp. 71–3). As well as representing a waste of materials, they all represent a waste of energy, technology and manpower. Though the purpose these products all once served is obvious, it is less easy to understand the purpose of packaging when all the consumer apparently has to do is to remove something from around a product and throw it away. Yet packaging has become an essential part of the consumer society. Many products reach us from considerable distances: packaging ensures that they travel safely and undamaged. Some yoghurt cartons, for example, are designed to stack one on top of the other so that the lids are unbroken in transit. Aerosols have substantial plastic caps so that they do not blast off their contents in transit. Packaging is also the way most goods are sold in self-service stores; you buy by the appearance of the pack because you cannot see the contents. The packaging also provides a surface for all the information required by the laws outlined in chapter 7: the weight, name, manufacturer, description, ingredients, etc. required by the Weights and Measures Act, the Food and Drugs Act, the Labelling of Food Regulations, and so forth.

Hygiene is another reason for packaging. Milk was once trundled through city streets in large containers open to dust and filth; then it was poured out on the doorstep into whatever the household had ready – open bowl, or dirty jug, perhaps. Now it is delivered in bottles, clean and free of germs, and in set quantities. Packaging is in fact part of the very considerable increase in the hygienic standards of foodstuffs, toiletries and many of the products we buy.

Packaging also makes buying a particular quantity very convenient. Though one can buy potatoes loose, prepacked they make a neater package to carry home. It is a distinct advantage to buy oil prepacked. Some products, indeed, would hardly exist without packaging; deodorants, hair spray, lipsticks, cassettes, are examples. Cassettes actually rely on the packaging to sell them; without the packaging customers would not know what music they contained.

There is yet another reason for packaging: to stop stealing. Shoplifting is a crime as old as the practice of displaying goods for sale, but it has become an acute problem with the spread of self-service and with retailers' anxiety about profit margins: shoplifting erodes profits, so they are naturally anxious to restrict it. Thus some products are deliberately 'overpackaged' to make them more difficult to steal. A small item like a packet of razor blades can easily be slipped into a pocket or bag: fixed to a big piece of card and covered with plastic it is less easy to hide away.

Finally, packaging uses glass, paper, plastic and metals. Solutions to the problem, none of them entirely satisfactory, are discussed on pp. 71–3.

ENERGY

The consumer society is based on a growing demand for energy in the form of transport, fuel, heat (or air conditioning in warm climates) and power to drive machinery in the home as well as power to drive the machinery which makes those consumer goods. Over the period 1968 to 1978, the total volume of traffic increased by 40 per cent. Average household electricity consumption in England and Wales rose from 3710 to 4180 units while demand for gas for domestic consumers in the United Kingdom rose from 238 therms to 551 over the same period. One effect is higher standards of comfort and mobility; another result is the consumption of fuels which can never be recovered. These points come home to us with particular force when the price of coal or oil causes inconvenience and rising prices as well as international economic problems.

These are the points the consumer notices first: so far it is in cars that low fuel consumption is being sought, and in industry and in homes that conservation measures are being applied and to a limited extent; many companies now have an energy manager. Energy-saving principles could be applied more widely to products like electrical appliances, and more extensively still to schools and hospitals. It needs consumer pressure, usually prompted more by rising prices than any dawning responsibility, to encourage energy-saving changes in design and the use of materials.

OBSOLESCENCE

Products inevitably age and the rate of ageing depends to a large extent on design and manufacture. If thinly coated metal panels are used for a car or a cooker, the product will show signs of wear soon enough for its owners to want to buy a replacement: the materials and technology are wasted. The same applies to most products; shoes and clothes are good examples. Manufacturers tell us that people do not want products to last a long time, that they want change. Manufacturers also point out that the cost of a completely rust-proof car or an everlasting pair of shoes would be very high. In any case, consumers would not want them; they like a change. So in theory a balance is struck between what the manufacturers can make and what the people are prepared to pay. In practice manufacturers design to a price, and customers pay without knowing what that means in terms of materials, design or construction. Inevitably, what a manufacturer calls a product's 'design life' is called 'planned obsolescence' by consumers faced with a product which breaks sooner than they expected, which they cannot get repaired, and for which spares are 'no longer being made'.

The preference for newness which many consumers have, and not only the young, is another aspect of 'obsolescence'. Such is the ingrained dissatisfaction with possessions that no sooner is one thing bought than something else appears which seems slightly better. This process is assisted by advertisers stressing 'new, improved' and also by the continuous movement of fashion, which applies to cars, food, holidays and electrical appliances just as much as to clothes, shoes, record stars, and films, and makes consumer responsibility almost invisible to the majority of consumers.

The relationship between people pressing for 'new' and manufacturers producing something 'new' is never clear and can be discussed endlessly; it is moreover an important element in consumer choice as well as in consumer dissatisfaction. It creates employment, new technology and profits, as well as waste of old technology and materials when the discarded products are thrown away.

SOME POSSIBLE SOLUTIONS

Just as the pressures towards new products and the wastage of old ones are complex, and the responsibility must be shared between consumers and producers, so too the problems of waste materials are complicated and the responsibility for solutions obscure. Yet waste is a resource, which can up to a point be utilized. Moreover, as an important aspect of consumer responsibility it has a place in consumer education.

The reuse of industrial waste – from manufacturing consumer goods like tin cans and cars for example – is more highly organized than the utilization of domestic waste. Plastic waste straight from the factory can be recycled when it is clean and all of the same type and specification: it is almost impossible to reuse domestic plastic waste, when it is a jumble of many different kinds, usually dirty and connected with other materials.

Some materials actually require a percentage of the waste product in manufacture: the steel industry for example relies to a large extent on scrap steel for making new steel, so that an industry has developed whereby scrap metal merchant collect old cars, crush and bale them, and sell them back to the steel mills. Newsprint and kraft (heavy-duty cardboard) contain a proportion of waste paper; glass contains a proportion of cullet, or old glass.

Domestic waste presents many more problems. It is dirty and jumbled together, so that it has to be re-sorted before it can be reused. Most local authorities in fact use it for landfill – along coast lines, in mine shafts and in old brick fields. But suitable places for dumping are becoming scarce, and this system is in any case a waste of resources, particularly of those in diminishing supply.

The alternatives to dumping exist, but most are experimental. There is a certain amount of pressure to sort and reuse materials and to find solutions to the problems of household waste, but this work is still relatively insignificant and has little impact. However it may well develop in the future: it is a useful exercise, in pressure group activities and local authority economics, for a class to find out what is happening locally and what the arguments are against implementing some of these proposals.

Waste can for example be used to generate electricity. Domestic waste is taken from all over north London to the incineration station at Edmonton, where it is burned to produce electricity which can be fed into the grid. The system could be adapted for use in some of the older outdated power stations in urban areas, which are instead being dismantled and replaced by new ones in rural areas. These require fuels like oil, coal and uranium which are finite, expensive and introduce other more serious social and environmental problems. Improvements in technology are required to avoid environmental pollution from the fumes emitted by burning household waste, but at a time when we are becoming conscious of using up finite resources, here is a way of using up an almost constantly renewable source of fuel.

Another system has been developed by the Warren Spring government laboratories at Stevenage. Household waste is collected and sorted to remove metals, which are sold to scrap merchants. Glass is also removed and used to make new glass. The rest is pulverized into a fine ash which can be burnt as fuel in power stations to generate electricity. This system has been adopted by a few local authorities on an experimental basis, e.g. in Chichester and Newcastle upon Tyne.

RECYCLING AND RECLAMATION

Some local authorities have adopted different waste collection and recycling systems: in Newcastle upon Tyne tin cans are removed from household waste, converted back into steel and tin, and sold for reuse. Kirklees as an authority worked with Oxfam on a system whereby householders sorted their rubbish into different coloured sacks, so that paper, glass, cloth and metals could be sold to merchants for resale to the different industries which could use them. Oxfordshire participated in a bottle bank scheme, which has been adopted by other local authorities, whereby householders deposit old bottles in containers according to the colour of the glass, so that they can be resold to the glass-making industry, which can only reuse them once they have been sorted. Many local authorities also have 'amenity sites', where people can take bottles, paper, used car oil and even old cars and bedsteads.

Many schools have their own collection schemes to raise money, and indeed the voluntary organizations play an important part in waste collection and recycling. What they collect depends on the price and demand from merchants: waste paper, glass bottles, aluminium foil have all been collected, and have paid for mini-buses, outings for the elderly or for deprived children, and facilities for churches, youth groups and schools. Jumble sales, another popular fund-raising activity, are also a form of recycling.

CONSERVATION

These recycling and reclamation schemes are in their way conservation measures. But these have also to be seen in terms of energy conservation: by using public transport, walking or cycling rather than use a car or motorbike, by cutting down heat a few degrees, by limiting the use of appliances, especially room heaters, by increasing insulating and draught-proofing, and by all the other measures to cut down on heat loss and therefore on energy use – while cutting fuel bills at the same time.

Waste management and energy conservation are still in the early stages, yet they have an essential part of consumer education, of a genuine consumer responsibility for the future. It would be irresponsible to educate children without this perception of changing attitudes towards waste, materials, energy and energy sources.

TEACHING EXPERIENCES

The enthusiasm of children for waste collection, particularly when there is a benefit in view, has been channelled by many schools, though usually as an extra-curricular activity. However a Dartford teacher incorporated this concept into community studies for fourth and fifth years by organizing waste collection among them, with the object of taking the pensioners, for whom they cared as part of the course, on an outing paid for by the sale of the materials they had collected. In Denmark, children learn about conservation by learning how to patch and darn their clothes attractively. A north London home economics teacher incorporates energy concepts for second-year boys and girls by including energy and waste in relation to food, personal time and energy saving in relation to so-called labour-saving appliances, and energy in the home in terms of cost, comfort and conservation.

Resources

Reclamation and recycling

War on Waste: A Policy for Reclamation, Government green paper (1974) on the potential for waste reclamation. (0 10 157270 0)
First Report of the Waste Management Advisory Council (1976). Somewhat out-of-date, but contains useful statistics and information on percentage of different forms of waste, how industry handles them, the cost of savings, etc. (0 11 751007 6)
Material Gains: Reclamation, Recycling and Re-use, Christine Thomas (Earth Resources Research, 1979). Proposals for dealing with waste, and a guide to current practices.
London's Refuse Disposal. Free illustrated leaflet on the history and organization of waste disposal in the Greater London area. From the GLC Information Centre, County Hall, London SE1.
Save and Recycle: A Guide to Voluntary Waste Collection. Information about different types of waste and addresses of merchants. Free from the National Anti-Waste Programme, Room 449, Ashdown House, 123 Victoria Street, London SW1E 6RB,

who also produce a free *Directory of Waste Collections*.
Litter: An Environmental Project. Teaching kit for middle-school children produced by the Keep Britain Tidy Group, Bostel House, 37 West Street, Brighton BN1 2RE.
The Paper Chain, Christine Thomas (Earth Resources Research, 1977). On the reclamation and recycling of paper.
Packaging
Many Happy Returns: Glass Containers and the Environment, Richard Bate (Friends of the Earth, 1976).
Glass Recycling in the UK, 1973–76. Report by the Glass Manufacturers' Federation, 19 Portland Place, London W1N 4BH. Industry appraisal of the problems and potential. Slightly dated, but useful.
Glass View. Free quarterly from the Glass Manufacturers' Federation. Usually includes information on bottle banks and glass reclamation.

Energy conservation

Making the Most of Your Petrol: Save a little to save a lot. Free advice leaflet from Publications Division, Automobile Association, Fanum House, Basingstoke, Hants. RG21 2EA.
Energy in the Home. Open University short course on assessing energy output and costs of the home and how to insulate and save energy. Useful course materials.
Teachers' Resource List on Electricity Consumers and Conservation. The Electricity Consumers' Council (p. 58).
Two Games from British Gas: Save It and Be Safe At Home. Board games (one on energy saving) and teachers' notes for middle-school children. Free from the Education Liaison Officer. Room 414, British Gas, 326 High Holborn, London WC1V 7PT.

10   More resources and useful addresses

General reading

An essential for teaching consumer education in the United Kingdom is a subscription to *Which?* (pp. 55–6). The *Journal of Consumer Studies and Home Economics*, published quarterly by Blackwell Scientific Publications Ltd (0309 3891), provides useful and informative background material for consumer education teaching, as does the Open University *Consumer Decisions* short course.

There are of course many other aspects of consumer affairs which this handbook does not include: the subject expands daily and it is unlikely that anyone will be foolhardy enough to attempt an encyclopedia. However teachers may find that they are necessarily led further into certain topics – such as food, energy, labelling, and health and safety. What follows is, like the other resources recommended elsewhere in this book, a selective list which teachers appear to find helpful.

Food

Food From Waste, Adrian Walker. A proposal for saving money and resources both in the context of the UK and the global situation. Oxfam Public Affairs Unit, Parnell House, Wilton Road, London SW1. (0 85598 032X)

Changing Food Habits in the UK, Chris Wardle (Earth Resources Research, 1977). Appraisal of the factors affecting diet – social, economic and political. (0 905966 03 1)

Wastage in the UK Food System, Robin Roy (Earth Resources Research). Food consumption in the UK and the losses involved.

Energy

Education Service Catalogue, Education Liaison Officer, Room 414, British Gas, 326 High Holborn, London WC1V 7PT.
Understanding Electricity (catalogue), Electricity Council, 30 Millbank, London SW1P 4RD.
Solid Fuel Advisory Service, Room 565, Hobart House, Grosvenor Place, London SW1X 7AE.

Labelling

Home Laundering Consultative Council, 24 Buckingham Gate, London SW1 6LB. Free leaflet on the fabric labelling code.
Washing Sense (wall chart) on the international care labelling code. Education Unit, Lever Brothers Ltd, Lever House, 3 St James's Road, Kingston on Thames, KT1 2BA
International Textile Care Labelling Wash Codes (wall chart). Proctor & Gamble Educational Service, PO Box 1EE, Gosforth, Newcastle upon Tyne NE99 1EE.

Health and safety

Health Education Council, 78 New Oxford Street, London WC1A 1AH. Wide selection of free leaflets on smoking, teeth, care of the elderly and of children, alcoholism, etc. Obtainable in Scotland from: the Health Education Unit, 21 Lansdowne Crescent, Edinburgh EH12 5EH.

Many of the materials mentioned as resources have been produced by pressure groups with special interests; in this context, teachers might also like to look at the materials produced by manufacturers as 'educational' materials. Food features particularly strongly – sugar, sweets, dairy produce, etc. Teachers could use this as an exercise to consider the apparent confusion in manufacturers' minds between education and advertising.

Index

adult education, 12, 32
advertising, 18, 19, 20, 21, 22;
    Advertising Association, 22
Advice Centre Servicing Unit, 55
advice services, 16, 45
airport users' consultative
    committees, 59
applied science and technology,
    11
Approved Coal Merchants'
    Scheme, 59
auctions, 28

banks, 18, 28, 29, 30, 36, 38, 45;
    bank cards, 34; Bank
    Education Service, 38; bank
    loans, 34; bank overdraft, 34
betting shops, 28, 29, 30
Birmingham Settlement, 37
British Electrotechnical
    Approvals Board, 53, 64
British Rail, 57
British Standards Institution, 7,
    53, 64
building societies, 18, 28, 30, 36,
    45, 51
buses, 29
business studies, 10

cafés, 28, 29
car parks, 29
cash, 34; cash and carry, 25
Central Transport Consultative
    Committee, 59
check trading, 35
cheques, 34
cinemas, 28
Citizen's Advice Bureaux, 31, 38,
    48, 56-7, 65

clean air, 51; Clean Air Acts, 46
coal, 51
Codes of Practice, 44, 48
commerce, 10
Common Agricultural Policy, 50,
    60
communications, 3, 11–12
Competition Act, 45, 58
complaints departments, 61–2
conservation, 11, 73
consumer advice centres, 31, 38,
    48, 54, 55, 65
Consumer Consultative
    Committee, 60, 61
Consumer Credit Act, 28, 35, 38,
    45, 54
Consumer Credit Association, 38
consumer education in: Belgium,
    3, 6; Denmark, 74; France, 6;
    Ireland, 7; Philippines, 7;
    Portugal, 7; Scandinavia, 6;
    Spain, 7; West Germany, 6;
    United States, 6
consumer organizations, 52–3,
    55–60
consumer protection, 49–63
Consumer Protection Acts, 43, 46
consumer protection
    departments, 40, 54, 55, 64
consumer relations
    departments, 62
consumer representatives, 60–61
consumer safety, 50, 64;
    Consumer Safety Act, 43, 54;
    Consumer Safety Unit, 50
Consumer Standards Advisory
    Committee, 53, 57, 61
Consumers' Association, 37, 48,
    55–6, 64, 65

Consumers in the European Community Group, 57, 61
Co-operative Union, 12, 57
Cosmetic Safety Regulations, 46
counter service, 23
county courts, 40, 48
credit, 35, 36; credit account cards, 35; credit cards, 34, 36
CSE, 9, 12, 37

debt, 35
Department of Energy, 7, 51
Department of the Environment, 51
Department of Health and Social Security, 50
Department of Prices and Consumer Protection (see Department of Trade)
Department of Trade, 7, 47, 49, 51, 58, 64
Department of Transport, 51
department stores, 24
design and technology, 3, 9
direct sales, 27; Direct Sales and Services Association, 31
Director General of Fair Trading, 44, 45, 52
discount stores, 25
Domestic Coal Consumers' Council, 59, 66
doorstep selling, 27, 31
drama, 12
dry cleaners, 28

economic and public affairs, 10
Economic and Social Committee, 60
economics, 3, 10
education, 14
EEC harmonization programme, 46, 60
elderly consumers, 14, 27
electric appliances (codes of practice), 48
Electric Blanket Regulations, 43

electricity, 11, 14, 15, 29, 50, 51, 57–9, 67, 72, 77; consultative councils, 58
Electricity Acts, 46
Electricity Consumers' Council, 7, 59, 66, 75
energy, 11, 69, 73, 74, 77; conservation, 11, 73
English, 11
environment, 14, 51
Environment and Consumer Protection Service, 2, 60
environmental health officers, 26, 40, 54, 55, 61, 64; Environmental Health Officers' Association, 65
environmental studies, 11
ethics, 3
European Commission, 2, 6, 46, 50, 60
European Communities Act, 46
European Community, 2, 7, 46, 52, 60
European Parliament, 60

fabric science, 31
Fair Trading Act, 44–5, 48, 52, 55
family and community studies, 10
farm shops, 26
Fibre Content Regulations, 9, 46
Finance Houses Association, 38
Food Additives and Contaminants Committee, 50
Food and Drugs Acts, 9, 40–2, 53, 68
Food Hygiene (General) Regulations, 41
Food Standards Committee, 50
footwear (code of practice), 44

gas, 14, 15, 29, 51, 57–8, 69, 77; consumer councils, 58
Gas Acts, 46
GCE O and A levels, 9, 12
general science, 11

general studies, 10
geography, 11, 30
government, economics and commerce, 10

hairdressers, 28
handicraft, 9
harmonization, 46, 50, 60
Heating Appliance Regulations, 43
higher education, 32, 36
hire purchase, 34
history, 11
holidays, 15, 44
home economics, 9, 12, 20
housebound consumers, 26, 27
housing, 14, 15, 51
human biology, 11

industrial studies, 10
Institute of Practitioners in Advertising, 22
Institute of Trading Standards Administration, 64
International Organization of Consumers' Unions, 4

jumble sales, 28, 73

Labelling of Food Regulations, 9, 41–2, 48, 68
launderers and dry cleaners, 9, 44
law, 3, 12, 39–40; civil, 39–40; criminal, 39, 40–7
legal studies, 11
local authority, 31, 52, 53, 72
London Electricity Consultative Council, 66
low income consumers, 14, 33, 52

mail order, 16, 27, 44
management studies, 12
manufacturers, 18
marketing, 12, 18, 19, 21, 22
markets, 25, 29

mathematics, 3
media, 62
metrication, 52; Metrication Board, 52
milk floats, 26
Ministry of Agriculture, Fisheries and Food, 50, 64
mobile vans, 26
money, 17, 32–8
money lenders, 35, 45
Monopolies and Mergers Commission, 44, 45
mortgages, 34
motivations: conscious, 16; unconscious, 16–17
multiples, 24, 29

National Association of Citizens' Advice Bureaux, 56, 65
National Association of Women's Clubs, 57
National Consumer Council, 21, 22, 28, 35, 37, 48, 50, 52, 61, 64
National Consumer Project, 57
National Council of Women, 57
National Federation of Consumer Groups, 7, 56, 65
National Federation of Women's Institutes, 57
National Gas Consumers' Council, 58, 65
National Health Service, 14, 51
National Savings Committee, 14, 51
National Union of Townswomens' Guilds, 57
nationalized industry consumer councils, 50, 57–9, 61
none-examination syllabuses, 12
Northern Ireland Department of Commerce, 58
Northern Ireland Consumer Council, 52
Northern Ireland Electricity Consumers' Council, 59

North of Scotland Electricity
  Consultative Council, 59

obsolescence, 70
Office of Fair Trading, 7, 9, 31,
  38, 48, 52, 53, 55, 57, 63, 64
Open University, 12, 56, 75, 76

packaging, 67–9
parentcraft, 37
parents as consumers, 14, 15
party selling, 27
pensioners, 15
personal service, 24
physics, 11
pocket money, 33
politics, 3
post offices, 18, 28, 29, 36, 57;
  postal services, 11
Post Office Users' National
  Council, 59, 66
pre-retirement courses, 3, 12, 32
pressure groups, 14, 60
Prices Acts, 45
prisoners-consumer education
  for, 13, 35
private sales, 28

religious studies, 12
Restrictive Practices Court, 44
retailers, 18, 23, 28, 61–2

Sale of Goods Act, 40, 48
saving, 35, 36
school banks, 36, 37
schoolchildren, 32
science, 11
Scottish Consumer Council, 52,
  64
Scottish Development
  Department, 58
Scottish syllabuses, 9
second-hand cars (codes of
  practice), 48
second-hand shops, 28

self-service, 23, 24
services, 28, 29, 30
Sheriff Court, 40
shopping, 23–31; shopping
  habits, 16
shops, 29
small claims, 40, 48
social sciences, 11
social services, 14
social studies, 3, 11
sociology, 11
specialist shops, 24
South of Scotland Electricity
  Consultative Council, 59

tallymen, 27, 35, 45
teenagers, 14, 15, 17–20, 21, 26,
  32
television rental, 28
Toy Safety Regulations, 43
Trade Descriptions Acts, 42, 43,
  47, 48, 54
Trading Stamps Act, 45
trading standards departments,
  40, 54, 55, 61, 65
transport, 14, 15, 30, 51
travel agents, 28, 30

Unfair Contract Terms Act, 40
Unsolicited Goods and Services
  Act, 46

vocational training, 12

waste, 67, 71–3, 74, 76; waste
  collection, 14
weights and measures, 50;
  Weights and Measures Act,
  42, 54, 68
Welsh Consumer Council, 7, 48,
  52, 64
Which?, 55, 56, 65, 76
Workers' Education Association,
  12

For Product Safety Concerns and Information please contact our EU
representative GPSR@taylorandfrancis.com Taylor & Francis Verlag GmbH,
Kaufingerstraße 24, 80331 München, Germany

Printed and bound by CPI Group (UK) Ltd, Croydon, CR0 4YY

01/05/2025

01858370-0001